VICTORIA TOWER
TREASURES

[Whereas] the Lords Spirituall and ... Temporall and Commons assembled at Westminster lawfully fully and freely representing all the Estates of the People of this Realme did upon the thirteenth day of February in the yeare of our Lord One ... thousand six hundred eighty eight present unto ... their Majesties then called and knowne by the ... Names and Style of William and Mary Prince and Princesse of Orange being present in their proper persons A certaine Declaration in ... Writing made by the said Lords and Commons in the words following vizt Whereas the late King James the Second by the Assistance of diverse evill Counsellors Judges and Ministers imployed by him did endeavour to subvert and extirpate the Protestant Religion and the Lawes and Liberties of this Kingdome By assuming and exerciseing a power of Dispensing with ... and suspending of Lawes and the Execution of Lawes without Consent of Parliament By ... committing and prosecuting diverse worthy ... Prelates for humbly petitioning to be excused from concurring to the said assumed Power By issuing

VICTORIA TOWER TREASURES

from the
Parliamentary Archives

Caroline Shenton, David Prior
and Mari Takayanagi

HOUSES OF PARLIAMENT
PARLIAMENTARY ARCHIVES

© Parliamentary Copyright House of Lords 2010

First published in Great Britain in 2010 by
the Parliamentary Archives

ISBN 978-0-9567363-07

British Library Cataloguing-in-Publication Data
A catalogue record is available from the British Library

Photography by Prudence Cuming Associates
Designed by Libanus Press Ltd, Marlborough
Printed by Hampton Printing (Bristol) Ltd

Cover: Death Warrant of Charles I, 1649
Frontispiece: Bill of Rights, 1689

Contents

From The Lord Speaker

and

The Speaker of the House of Commons

The decision of the Clerk of the Parliaments in March 1497 to retain at Westminster, and not transfer to Chancery, the bills or 'Original Acts' that had received Royal Assent in the most recent session of Parliament began a tradition of record keeping at Westminster of which both Houses can be justifiably proud.

It is a tradition that at times has been at the mercy of events. The Great Fire of October 1834 ranks as the most catastrophic of these since it destroyed almost all of the old Palace of Westminster and, in the process, most of the records of the House of Commons. The fire did, however, prove to be a turning point in the history of record keeping at Westminster. Charles Barry's designs for the new Palace of Westminster included provision for purpose-built accommodation for the storage of Parliament's records in the form of the Victoria Tower, the 150th anniversary of which this publication marks.

Since the completion of the Victoria Tower in May 1860 there have been other achievements which have contributed to the preservation of the archives of both Houses. The establishment of the House of Lords Record Office in 1946 and the subsequent renovation of the Tower represented a major step forward in the provision of professional support and modern facilities for record keeping in the Palace. These developments also provided a solid foundation for the work that the Parliamentary Archives does today to manage, preserve and provide access to Parliament's records.

The 150 treasures that have been selected for this book are a testimony to the archival riches which are preserved in the Victoria Tower. We hope that you will enjoy learning both about them, and the history and work of Parliament, which they so vividly illustrate.

Lord Speaker

Speaker

Introduction

The survival and preservation of the archives of both Houses of Parliament is inextricably bound up with the history of the Palace of Westminster. The collections that have come down to us – a snapshot of which is provided in this book – will be forever scarred by the fire of October 1834, but it was the fact that the records of the House of Lords were stored in the Jewel Tower on the perimeter of the old Palace which helped ensure their survival whilst the records of the House of Commons, kept elsewhere, were destroyed. The inclusion, in the designs for the new Palace, of the Victoria Tower as a purpose-built repository for the storage of Parliament's records was a landmark decision in the history of archiving at Westminster, which has subsequently enabled the application of professional skills to the preservation of our documentary heritage for the benefit of the nation.

Parliament's records began to accumulate at Westminster in 1497. The Jewel Tower was used to house the records of the House of Lords from the late sixteenth century and, by the nineteenth century, there were also record stores in a basement under the Lords. The records of the House of Commons were stored in and around its Journal Office and, from 1828, probably also near its new library. Following the catastrophic fire of 1834 the Government announced a competition to design a new Palace of Westminster, including the stipulation that the building should contain *'Fireproof Repositories for Papers and Documents'*. The prize-winning neo-gothic design by the architect Sir Charles Barry featured his response to that challenge: an enormous stone square tower over the 'Royal Entrance', soaring 98m (323ft) to the base of its flagstaff, itself 22m (72ft) high. Inside, a cast-iron spiral staircase of 553 steps linked 12 floors and, on most levels, there were eight strongrooms with heavy iron doors.

The first stone of this monumental building was laid by Barry's wife on 22 December 1843. Originally called 'The King's Tower' after William IV, it was later renamed after his successor. The Victoria Tower was to become an unmistakeable part of the London skyline and a dominant feature of the architecture of the Houses of Parliament. During the State Opening of Parliament the Monarch enters the Palace of Westminster through the Sovereign's Entrance, directly underneath the Tower. Barry believed that it would be the Victoria Tower, rather than the Clock Tower housing Big Ben, which would catch the popular imagination and be his lasting monument. He died in May 1860, the same month that the Tower was completed. The brass on Barry's tomb in Westminster Abbey is engraved with an elevation of the Victoria Tower and a ground plan of the Palace. The Union Jack was flown for the first time from its summit for his funeral on 22 May 1860.

Following the Tower's completion, the records of the House of Lords were gradually transferred from their home in the Jewel Tower and the basements along the river terraces. After 1927 they were joined by most of the post-fire records of the House of Commons. In 1937 the Clerk of the Parliaments, Sir Henry Badeley, initiated a survey of the contents of the Tower and the resulting report revealed the need for full-time staff to manage the archives. The Second World War (during which time the contents of the Tower were evacuated to the country) interrupted implementation of the report. In 1946, following the return of the records to the Tower, the House of Lords Record Office was established to care for its contents and to provide public access to them. With this assurance, the original manuscript Journals of the Commons, dating from 1547, were deposited by the authority of the Speaker in 1957.

The Tower – a historic treasure in its own right – has undergone a number of facelifts and improvements itself since 1860. Within a few years of its completion, the magnesian limestone used for its external walls began to succumb to the pollution of nineteenth-century London. By the 1920s significant fragments of stone were falling off and considerable quantities could simply be removed by hand. In 1926, restoration of the exterior stonework of the Tower began under the auspices of the Ministry of Works. This was an enormous undertaking and had to be discontinued during the Second World War, during which the roof of the Tower was attacked with incendiary bombs but survived. The scaffolding, however, remained in place and the work was eventually completed in 1953.

By 1948 the Tower's interior was also causing concern. The establishment of a professional archive service within Parliament had led to a greater appreciation of the need for a correct storage environment, but initial plans to install air-conditioning within the repository rooms were overtaken by the realisation that the structure of the Tower was deficient and that extensive work was required to transfer the 276-ton weight of the roof to the outside walls. During the renovation work the interior of the Tower was totally transformed and seven new lightweight floors were constructed in the upper part of the Tower. In addition, air-conditioning plant, a lift, six miles of new steel shelving and smoke detectors were installed. The building work was completed in October 1962 and the Tower was reopened by Viscount Hailsham, Leader of the House of Lords, on 3 July 1963, with the hope that '*this new building may have a long and distinguished career . . . in the service of Parliament, history and culture*'.

Between 1988 and 1989 another detailed inspection of the external masonry of the Victoria Tower was carried out. The survey revealed that, although the stonework was generally in a good condition, continuing pollution had further damaged the Tower's fabric. A second major programme of stonework restoration in the Tower's history necessitated the construction of an intricate web of scaffolding around the Tower. The result was one of the largest independent scaffolds in Europe, comprising 68 miles of scaffold tube and some 125,000 fittings. The process of cleaning and repairing the stonework was completed in 1993. By the late 1990s, the 1950s air-conditioning system was failing to comply with modern standards for the storage of archival material. Between 2000 and 2004 the system was replaced and fire protection enhanced. Environmental conditions in the Victoria Tower now meet British Standard BS5454: the temperature is maintained at a constant 16.5°C with a relative humidity of 55%.

The 150th anniversary of the Victoria Tower has provided an ideal opportunity to select 150 treasures, from the three million records currently stored in the Tower, for this celebratory book. Some are already well-known, others less so. It will come as no surprise that the first document in the book is the first of those Acts which were retained at Westminster in 1497, nor that Acts are a prominent feature of the remaining 149 treasures, given the impact that legislation has had on the people and communities of the United Kingdom, and also on other parts of the world, over a period of over 500 years. In addition, a selection of this kind could not ignore some of the key constitutional documents that have shaped the nation, such as the Death Warrant of Charles I, the Draft Declaration of Rights and the Acts which reformed the electoral system. What is revealing, however, is the insight that some of the other selected documents provide about the lives of ordinary people who came into contact with Parliament – whether it was the watermen working at the Parliament stairs in 1645, irate colonists in America in 1774, the inhabitants of Manchester who petitioned against the Slave Trade in 1806, or the women who unfurled a banner from the Ladies' Gallery in the House of Commons in 1908.

Archivists are trained to take the long view and, in compiling a book like this, we have been particularly aware of the dedication of the generations of archivists and archivally-minded Clerks before us who, over the centuries, have safeguarded, identified, cared for, and made available to their own and future generations the records of Parliament. Any selection from such a rich, varied and internationally important collection is bound to involve difficult choices about what to include. So, if one or two of your favourites are not here, we are confident you will still find a few familiar friends and maybe some new discoveries. And, if you are coming to our collections for the first time, we hope you find it a fascinating and thought-provoking tour.

Caroline Shenton
David Prior
Mari Takayanagi

November 2010

...e kynge oure souereign lord present yere som...

...n tyme passed be by the saide corporacion of mak...

...ony apprentice but if the partye make dyspost...

...of apprentice the said corporacion to hol...

...e the ympouisshyng of the inhabitauntes of...

...lordes spirituall and temporall and of the...

...of thafforesaid corporacion within yere...

...e to kepe apprentice shall by this present...

...cion soo that he passe not thre at on...

...a ordynances afore made to the contrarye...

1 *An Act for taking of Apprentices to make Worsteds in the County of Norfolk*, 12 Henry VII, c.1, 1497
Parliamentary Archives, HL/PO/PU/1/1497/12H7n1

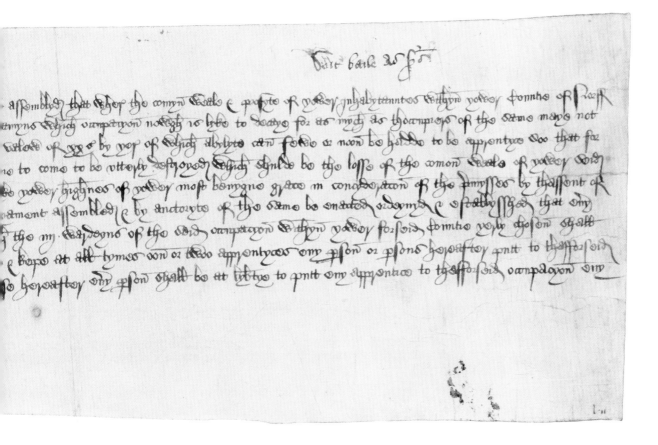

Pleasith it yo[ur] hyghnes and youre [...]
[...]realme by reason off bryngyng of ffren[...]
Cappmakers and hatt makers beyng In ha[...]

Where as off late yo[ur] hyghnes by the [...]
holden at Westm[inster] dyd establisshe and [...]
this yo[ur] Realme shulde be solde A bone[...]
of syd And that apon payne that e[...]
Acte if it were duly obserued and kept [...]
is occupied the most p[ar]tie by makyng[...]
beyng only by makyng of the said [...]
and pressers off Cappes and no Capp[...]
by the same / to the greate releef and [...]
Workes within this youre tolbne [...]
into the Countie to ffayers and me[...]
sell frenche Cappes and hatte, disguysed [...]

The 16th Century

Parchment Perfect

The Parliamentary Archives holds one of the largest accumulations of parchment documents in the United Kingdom outside the National Archives. All Acts of Parliament are either written or printed on this treated animal hide which is usually obtained from goats or sheep. Many other records in the post-medieval period were submitted to Parliament in this format, in an era before paper became cheap and widespread. Sometimes, thrifty petitioners would ensure they used the entire animal-shaped skin rather than cutting it into rectangles which involved wastage. Parchment is also a very durable and flexible medium, which can be folded and manipulated into various shapes, as evidenced by the use of multiple seal tags on a petition from the reign of Henry VIII.

2 Parchment petitions, 1531
Parliamentary Archives,
HL/PO/JO/ 10/3/178/4, 8

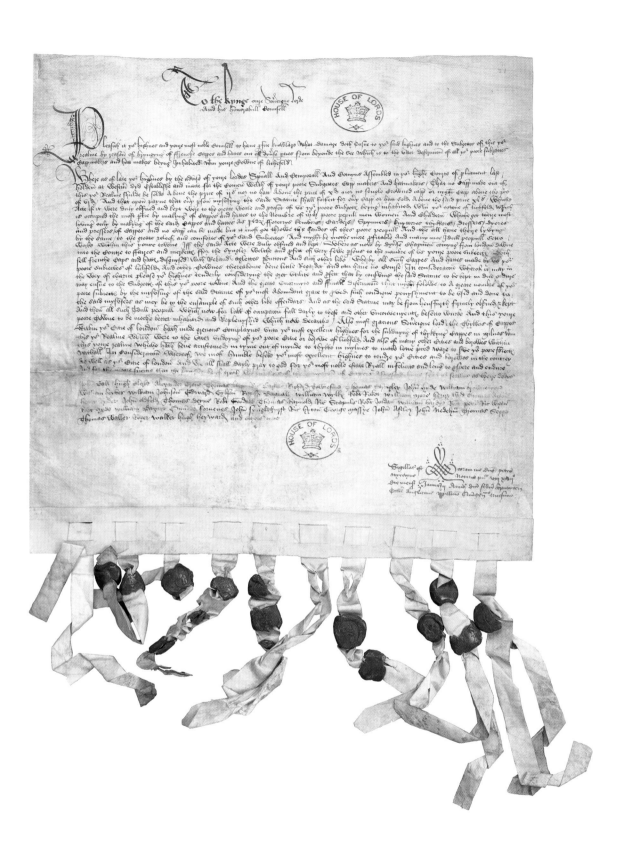

The Business of Tudor Parliaments

During the course of the sixteenth century, the proceedings of each House began to be recorded in a new manner. Draft minutes, written by the Clerks at the Table of each House when business was underway, were later turned into fair copy and bound together to create authoritative accounts of each daily sitting. These became known as the Journals. Despite the growth in Parliament's importance which this bureaucratic innovation suggests, things were not always so simple, and a monarch as powerful as Elizabeth I could still easily influence the business and manipulate the opinions of both Houses. Two examples are given here. In 1573 Elizabeth prorogued Parliament in order to avoid giving her assent to a bill which had been passed to deprive Mary Queen of Scots of the right of succession to the English Crown. And, on 21 January 1581, the Commons voted through a day of public fasting, prayer and preaching for Members. Three days later, the Queen sent a message to the Commons expressing her extreme displeasure and '*reproving the undutiful Proceedings of this House*'. The Speaker grovellingly declared himself '*to be very sorry for the Error that happened here, in this House upon Saturday last, in resolving to have a Publick Fast*'.

3 Original manuscript Journal of the House of Lords, 1510
Parliamentary Archives, HL/PO/JO/1/1

4 Original manuscript Journal of the House of Commons, 1547
Parliamentary Archives, HC/CL/JO/1/1

5 Royal Commission
for the prorogation of
Parliament, 12 October 1573
Parliamentary Archives,
HL/PO/JO/10/3/295/3

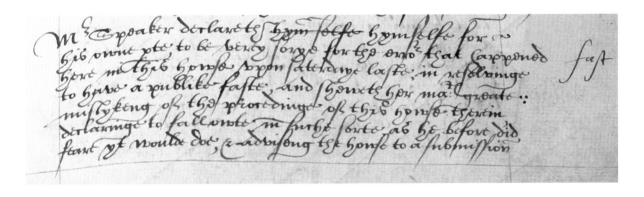

6 Elizabeth I's rebuke, original manuscript Journal of the House of Commons, 24 January 1581
Parliamentary Archives, HC/CL/JO/1/2

Tudor Acts

Under the Tudor monarchs, Parliament was used as a means of enacting legislation that fundamentally shaped the civil and religious life of the nation as well as the lives of ordinary citizens.

An Act of 1511 restricted the right to use the cross-bow to lords and owners of land to the yearly value of 300 marks (£200). Its object was to encourage others to use the longbow, which was still regarded as important for the defence of the kingdom. In 1534 the Act of Supremacy established the English monarch as the official head of the Church of England, supplanting the power of the Pope in Rome. This had its origins in the Pope's refusal to grant Henry VIII a divorce from Catherine of Aragon and, in creating such close bonds between the Monarch and the Church, the Act made support for the papacy or Catholicism a challenge to Royal authority and therefore an act of treason punishable by death.

The union of England and Wales resulted from two Acts passed between 1536 and 1542. The legislation defined Welsh parliamentary representation at Westminster and imposed English law and the English language upon the Welsh.

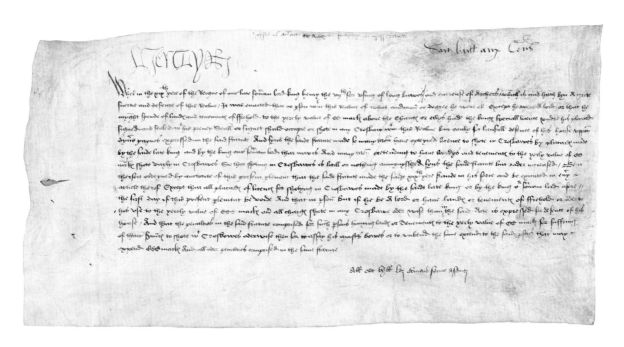

7 *An Act against shotting in Cross-bows*, 3 Henry VIII, c. 13, 1511
Parliamentary Archives, HL/PO/PU/1/1511/3H8n13

8 *An Act concerning the King's Highness to be Supreme Head of the Church of England, and to have Authority to reform and redress all Errors, Heresies and Abuses in the same, 26 Henry VIII, c. 1, 1534*
Parliamentary Archives, HL/PO/PU/1/1534/26H8n1

9 *An Act for Laws and Justice to be ministered in Wales in like Form as it is in this Realm*, 27 Henry VIII, c. 26, 1536
Parliamentary Archives, HL/PO/PU/1/1535/27H8n24

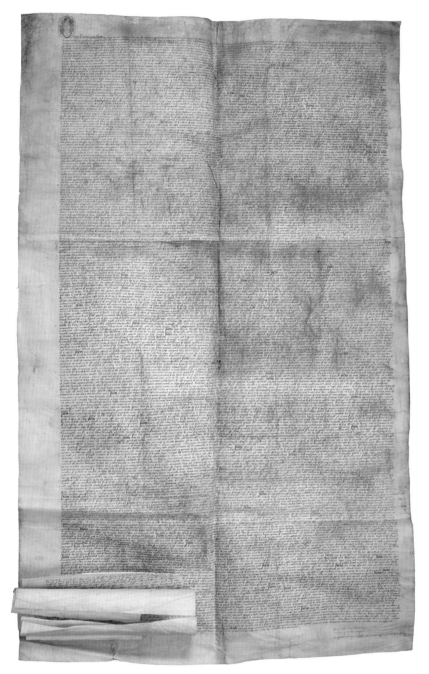

10 *An Act for certain Ordinances
in the King's Majesty's Dominion
and Principality of Wales,*
34 & 35 Henry VIII, c. 26, 1542
Parliamentary Archives,
HL/PO/PU/1/1542/34&35H8n25

Trials and Executions

The turbulent nature of life at Court in the sixteenth century is reflected in legislation that both Henry VIII and his daughter Elizabeth used against their enemies. The reign of Henry VIII was marked by the King's successful attempts to end two of his marriages on grounds of treason. An example of this is the Act of Attainder relating to his fifth wife, Katharine Howard, which was passed by the House of Lords in February 1542. Five years later, in January 1547, Howard's uncle, the 3rd Duke of Norfolk, was attainted for treason but escaped execution on account of the death of the King. During the reign of Henry's daughter Elizabeth, Mary Queen of Scots was tried and found guilty of plotting to kill the Queen. She was executed at Fotheringhay Castle on 8 Feb 1587. The original record of the trial was transmitted to Sir Christopher Hatton, Lord Chancellor, on 7 March 1588. At about the same time a copy was made for preservation in the archives of Parliament and, since the sealed copy is now lost, this is the most authoritative record.

11 *An Act concerning the Attainder of the late Queen Katharine and her Complices*, 33 Henry VIII, c.21, 1542
Parliamentary Archives, HL/PO/PU/1/1541/37H8n33

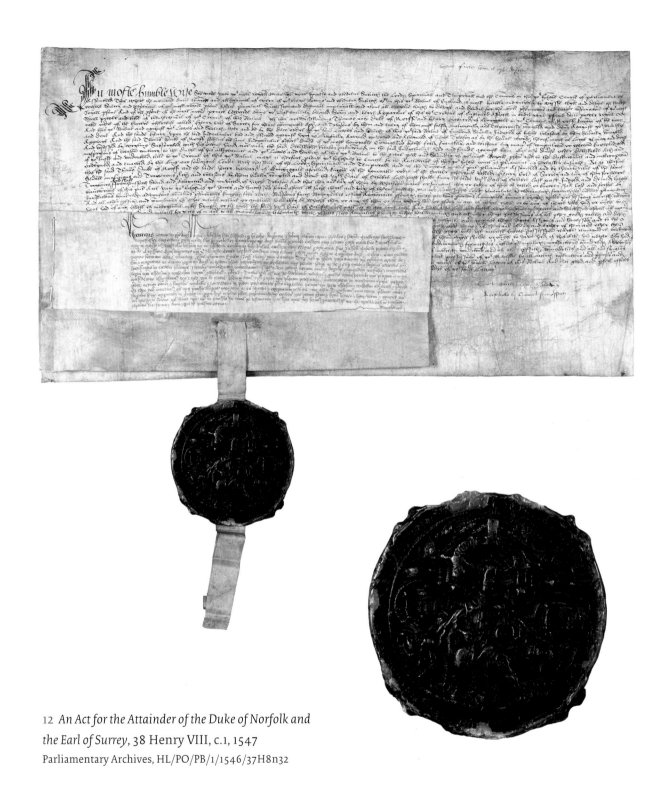

12 *An Act for the Attainder of the Duke of Norfolk and the Earl of Surrey*, 38 Henry VIII, c.1, 1547

Parliamentary Archives, HL/PO/PB/1/1546/37H8n32

Dua Regina mandauit Reuerendissimo in Christo p[at]ri ...

Anglie primati et metropolitano et v[vir]o de priuato Consilio / no[stro]

Bromley militi D[omi]no Cancellario Anglie alteri de priuato [Consilio]

Willimo d[omi]no Burghley d[omi]no Thesaurar[io] Ang[lie], alti de priuato [Consilio]

verba, **Elizabeth** dei gra[tia] Ang[lie] Fra[n]cie et Hib[er]nie Regina fi[dei ...]

mi[nis]tro Christo p[at]ri Joh[ann]i Cantuar[iensi] Archiep[iscop]o tot[ius] Ang[lie] p[ri]mati et metrop[olitano]

A[c] predc[t]o et fideli n[ost]ro Thome Bromley militi d[omi]no Cancella[rio]

n[ost]ro, Predilectoq[ue] et fideli n[ost]ro Willimo d[omi]no Burghley d[omi]no Thesa[urario]

n[ost]ro, Necnon charissimo Consangu[i]neo n[ost]ro, Willimo marchioni [...]

charissimoq[ue] Consangu[i]neo n[ost]ro Edwardo Comiti Oxon march[...]

Necnon charissimo Consangu[i]neo n[ost]ro Georgio Comiti Salop[ie ...]

Consilio n[ost]ro, A[c] charissimo Consangu[i]neo n[ost]ro Henrico Com[iti ...]

charissimo Consangu[i]neo n[ost]ro Henrico Comiti verb[...] ulti de p[riuato]

Consangu[i]neo n[ost]ro Willimo Comiti Wigorn[iensi] ulti d[omi]nor[um] parliamenti,

Edwardo Comiti Rotel[and], alteri d[omi]nor[um] parliamenti, A[c] chariss[imo]

Cumbr[...] ulti d[omi]nor[um] parliamenti, Necnon charissimo Consan[guineo]

magistro ordinarum n[ost]rar[um] ulti de priuato Consilio n[ost]ro, Chariss[imo]

Pembrook ulti d[omi]nor[um] parliamenti Necnon charissimo Cons[anguineo]

magistro Eqno[rum] n[ost]ror[um] ulti de priuato Consilio n[ost]ro, A[c] chari[ssimo]

Comiti Lincoln ulti d[omi]nor[um] p[ar]liamenti, Necnon charissimo Co[nsanguineo]

momtagne ulti d[omi]nor[um] p[ar]liamenti, Predilectoq[ue] et fideli n[ost]ro [...]

n[ost]ro Ang[lie] ulti de priuato Consilio n[ost]ro, A[c] predc[t]o et fideli [n[ost]ro ...]

Camerar[io] n[ost]ro ulti de priuato Consilio n[ost]ro, Necnon predc[t]o et fi[deli]

ulti d[omi]nor[um] parliamenti, A[c] predc[t]o et fideli n[ost]ro Edwardo d[omi]no [...]

predc[t]o et fideli n[ost]ro Edwardo d[omi]no Morley ulti d[omi]nor[um] p[ar]liamenti,

d[omi]no Gardiano q[ui]nq[ue] portuum n[ost]ror[um] ulti de priuato Consilio n[ost]ro [...]

Stafford ulti d[omi]nor[um] p[ar]liamenti, A[c] predc[t]o et fideli n[ost]ro, A[...]

Necnon predc[t]o et fideli n[ost]ro, Joh[ann]i d[omi]no Lumley ulti d[omi]nor[um] p[ar]liamenti [...]

The 17th Century

The Peerage

Until 1876 the House of Lords was occupied solely by hereditary Lords Temporal (peers of the realm who had inherited their right to sit there) and the Lords Spiritual (bishops who sat as a result of their position in the established Church).

Garter King of Arms was the herald traditionally concerned with the precedence (that is their listing in seniority) of peers. From 1628 he laid on the Table of the House of Lords, at the beginning of each new parliament or session, a parchment roll of the Lords Temporal in order of precedence. This practice continued until 1966.

Where there was dispute about inheritance to a peerage the matter fell within the jurisdiction of the House of Lords, which gave judgment on such peerage claims. William Knollys, Viscount Wallingford, was created Earl of Banbury in 1626 by Letters Patent which gave him precedence over other earls created by the King. The House of Lords protested but eventually agreed to it on the understanding that the Earl had no heirs. At the Restoration an heir appeared and the House, in investigating his claim, appropriated the patent as evidence. The portrait of Charles I is one of the best surviving examples of contemporary patent illumination.

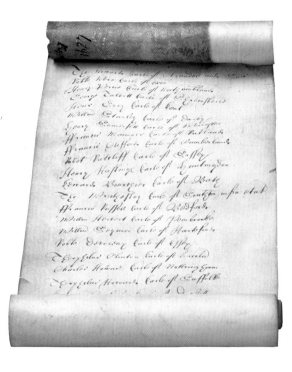

Left:
14 The first Garter's Roll, 1628
Parliamentary Archives, HL/PO/JO/7/1

Opposite:
15 Letters Patent of the Earl of Banbury, 18 August 1626
Parliamentary Archives, HL/PO/JO/10/3/178A

Stou
Offic
Pretel
et ex
Vn
serui
totumit
et liberatorum per multos Annos summu
NOS her omnia multaquē alia p
nostro habuimus, quomodo nos aliquid u
nostram regram celebrandam, aliquos c̄
detrevernimus, vtpotē qui antea ordinē p

Luxury Goods

The Parliamentary Archives holds many pieces of legislation relating to the regulation or encouragement of particular trades. Also among its collections, however, are other records which shed light on conspicuous consumption in the seventeenth century. These Letters Patent, incorporating the Company of Beaver Hat and Capmakers, were drawn up in 1638 and later presented to the House of Lords. The decorative border includes charming illustrations of the aquatic rodents as well as fur hats. Another document mentions the establishment of a novel refreshment facility at Westminster serving coffee, tea and chocolate for Members during sittings of the House of Commons.

16 Letters Patent incorporating the Company of Beaver Hat and Cap makers, 19 February 1638
Parliamentary Archives, HL/PO/JO/10/3/176/4

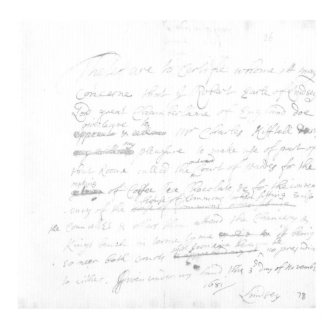

17 Permission to make coffee in the
Palace of Westminster, 3 November 1681
Parliamentary Archives, LGC/5/1/26

Petitioning Parliament

The submission of a petition has, for centuries, been a mechanism whereby individuals or bodies can attempt to influence the proceedings of Parliament. The petition to the House of Lords from the watermen working next to the Palace of Westminster in 1645, and that from Cuthbert Morley and Bernard Grenvile in 1667, are examples of petitions relating to the grievances of private individuals. The watermen are concerned at the decayed state of the causeway leading down from the stairs which is affecting their ability to operate; Morley and Grenvile are involved in a dispute over an estate. In contrast, the purpose of the Mayor of Norwich's petition in 1697 to the Lords was to object to the Parliamentary Elections Regulation Bill.

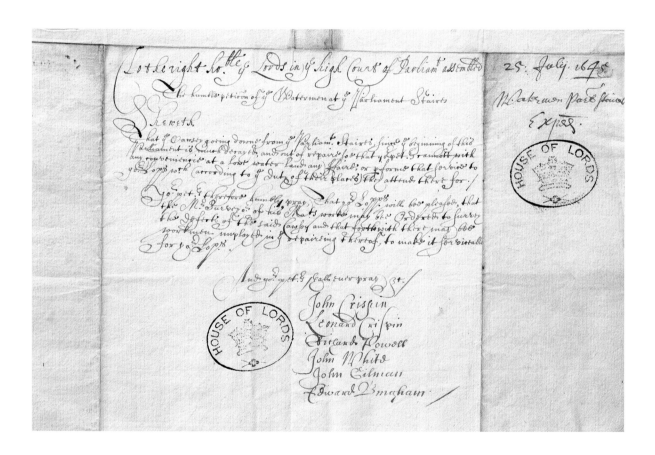

18 Petition of the watermen at the Parliament stairs, 25 July 1645
Parliamentary Archives, HL/PO/JO/10/1/190

19 Petition of Cuthbert
Morley and Bernard
Grenvile, 16 November 1667
Parliamentary Archives,
HL/PO/JO/10/1/328/107

20 Petition of the Mayor
and Corporation of
Norwich, 23 January 1697
Parliamentary Archives,
HL/PO/JO/10/2/23B

Plots and Conspiracies

Plots against the ruling elite were not uncommon before the seventeenth century, but the plan by a group of Catholic conspirators in November 1605 to blow up the Chamber of the House of Lords during the State Opening of Parliament was an unprecedented attempt at destruction on a massive scale which, if successful, would have killed the King and members of his family, his ministers and many Members of both the Upper House and the House of Commons.

The discovery of 36 barrels of gunpowder beneath the House of Lords and the arrest of Guy Fawkes, who was using the alias John Johnson, was recorded in the margin of the Journal of the House of Commons on 5 November 1605. Shortly afterwards an Act was passed which made the 5th of November a day of thanksgiving.

Later in the century, fears of a Catholic conspiracy resurfaced both during the affair of the 'Popish Plot' (which was allegedly a plan to assassinate Charles II and replace him with his Catholic brother) and also shortly after the Glorious Revolution.

21 Original manuscript Journal of the House of Commons, 5 November 1605
Parliamentary Archives, HC/CL/JO/1/5

This last night one
Cellar under house
of Parlyament was
searched by Sir Tho.
Knevett, and one
Johnston servt to
Mr Thomas Percy
was there apprehended
who had plased
36. barrells of
gunpowder in the
vault under the
house with a
purpose to blown
it. and the whole
company, which
they should here
assemble.

Afterwards disse
they were
discovered to be
the plott.

Mr Door Harbott
Sir Geo. Moore
Sir Geo. Somer
Sir Wm Greud
Sir Tho. Ridg
Sir Jo. Heigh
Mr James
Sir Hert Hol
Mr James of
Sir Fergher
Mr Collecby
Mr Martin
Mr Edw. Manne
Mr Hossman

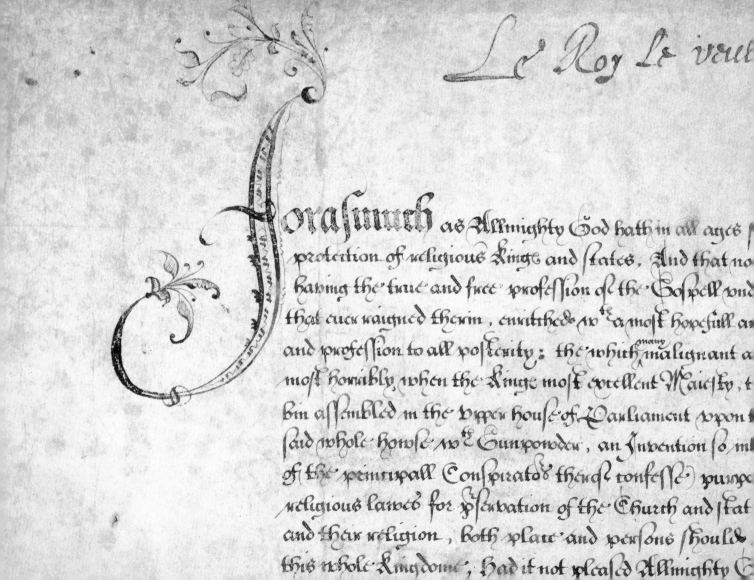

23 Anonymous letter concerning the 'Popish Plot', May 1679
Parliamentary Archives, HL/PO/JO/10/1/390B

24 Anonymous letter to the Marquess of Carmarthen alleging a second Gunpowder Plot, 20 November 1690
Parliamentary Archives, HL/PO/JO/10/1/429A

Crown and Parliament

Relations between Crown and Parliament reached crisis point during the reigns of James I and his son Charles I. Whilst James had established a good working relationship with the Scottish Parliament, this was not mirrored at Westminster following his succession to the English throne in 1603. Suspicions about the King's intentions, which were rooted in the issue of the Royal finances, led to the deadlock of the 'Addled' Parliament of 1614. By then Robert Cecil, referred to by James as his *little beagle*, and who had been responsible for the difficult task of managing the King's business in Parliament, was dead. In 1621 James forbade the House of Commons to discuss the matter of the proposed marriage of his son Charles to the daughter of the King of Spain on the grounds that it was not their concern. In response, on 18 December, a protestation concerning the privileges of the House was recorded in the journal of proceedings. In consequence the Clerk of the House was summoned before the King, who tore out the record of the protestation.

When Charles became King in 1625 the friction between Crown and Parliament continued. The reluctance of the 1626 Parliament to grant substantial funds for a military campaign, together with its impeachment of the King's favourite the Duke of Buckingham, led Charles to dissolve it. The subsequent levy by Charles of a non-parliamentary tax, and the imprisonment of those who refused to pay, triggered the drawing up of the Petition of Right by the Commons in 1628. The petition proclaimed, among other things, the illegality of taxation without parliamentary consent and arbitrary imprisonment. Although Charles accepted this curtailment of the Royal prerogative and the petition became an Act, suspicions remained about the King's interpretation of the episode and, after its dissolution the following year, Parliament did not meet for 11 years.

When the Long Parliament met in November 1640 Charles had to accept curtailments to his power, as well as the impeachment and execution of his chief minister, the Earl of Strafford, in 1641. During the next 12 months relations between Crown and Parliament broke down completely and in August 1642 the raising of the King's standard at Nottingham marked the start of the Civil War. After the decisive Royalist defeat at Naseby in June 1645 Charles fled the battlefield, leaving a cache of letters in cypher that fell into the hands of the Parliamentary army.

The trial of Charles I began in Westminster Hall on 20 January 1649. Before a High Court of Justice established by the House of Commons, which had recently been purged of Members unsympathetic to punishing the King and made up of 135 commissioners presided over by John Bradshaw, Charles was charged with having governed outside of the law and waging war on Parliament. Charles refused to plead and questioned the authority of the court. Despite this the trial went ahead; the King was found guilty of High Treason and a sentence of death by beheading was pronounced on 27 January. At the end of the trial a committee was appointed to prepare a record of the proceedings which was eventually presented to the Commons in December 1650. An engrossed version of the trial was sent to Chancery but came into possession of the House of Lords after the restoration of Charles II and has remained amongst the records of Parliament.

The warrant for the execution of Charles I is the most significant constitutional document held by the Parliamentary Archives and is perhaps the most dramatic of all records relating to English history. While some previous monarchs had met with premature and bloody deaths, none had been tried by a court set up by Parliament. The warrant seems to have been drawn up by the time the sentence was pronounced and between then and the 29th of January blank spaces were filled in and the signatures of 59 of the commissioners added, including that of Oliver Cromwell. The sentence was carried out on 30 January 1649 outside the Banqueting House in Whitehall. The Death Warrant remained in the hands of Colonel Hacker until 1660 when the House of Lords ordered him to surrender it into their custody.

25 Letter from James I to Robert Cecil, c.1607
Parliamentary Archives, HL/PO/JO/10/1/6A

26 Royal Commission for the
prorogation of Parliament,
16 November 1607
Parliamentary Archives,
HL/PO/JO/10/3/295/5

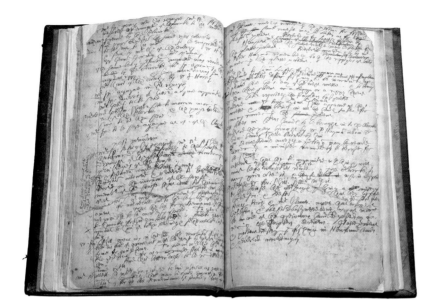

27 Original manuscript Journal of the House of Commons, 18 December 1621 (the 'torn Journal')
Parliamentary Archives, HC/CL/JO/1/11

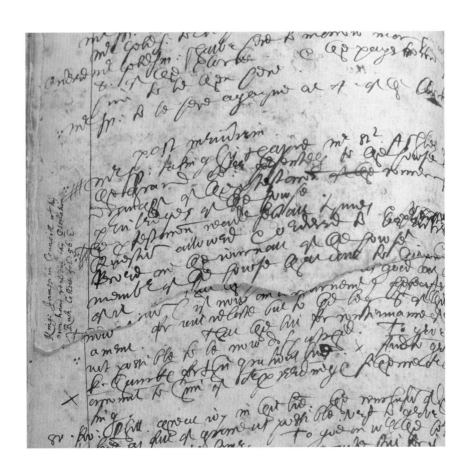

Right:

28 Diary of the Parliament of 1626 by
Sir Nathaniel Rich MP
Parliamentary Archives, MAN/66

Below:

29 *The Petition exhibited to His Majesty by the*
Lords Spiritual and Temporal, and Commons, in this
present Parliament assembled, concerning divers
Rights and Liberties of the Subject with the King's
Majesty's Royal Answer thereunto in Parliament
(the Petition of Right), 3 Charles I, c.1, 1628
Parliamentary Archives, HL/PO/PU/1/1627/3C1n2

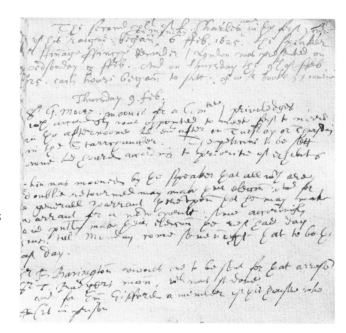

My Lords, I did yesterday satisfie the Justice of the Kingdome
by the pasing of the Bill of Attaindour against the Earle of
Strafford: but Mercie being as inherent & inseperable to a King
as Justice, I desyre, at this tyme, in some measure, to show that Lykewais, by suffering that vnfortunat Man to fullfill the naturall
curse of his Lyfe, in a close Imprisonment; yet so, that if euer he
make the least offer to escape, or offer, directlie or indirectlie to
medle in anie sorte of publike businesß, espetiallie with mee, by eather
meßadge or letter, it shall coste him his Lyfe, without further
Proceße: This, if it may bee done, without a discontentment to my
People, would be an vnspeacaple contentment to mee: To wch end,
as in the first place, I, by this letter, doe earnestlie desyre your ap=
probation ~~~~~~~ (& to endeare it the more, haue chosen him to cary
it, that of all your Howse, is most cleare to me) so I desyre that by
a conference, ye would endeauor to giue the Howse of Comõns,
contentment Lykewais: aßuring you, that the excersing of Mercy
is no more pleasing to me, then to see bothe my Howses of Par=
            contente
lament, ~~~~~~~ for my sake, that I should moderat the seueritie
                                will
of a Law, in so important a Case: I ~~~~ say, that your com-
                          intendit Mercie
plying with mee, in this my ~~~~~~~~~~~~~, shall make me
more willing, but certainelie, it will make me ~~~~~~~ more
          in granting
cheerfull ~~~~~~ your just Greeuances: but if no leße then his
Lyfe, cann satisfie my People, I must say Fiat Justitia: Thus
                                                          intensign
againe earnestlie recomending the consideration of my ~~~~~
unto you, I rest

If he must Dey, it wer a Charitie to   Your vnalterable affec=
repryue vntill Saterday   tionat frend
                                                         Charles R
Whythall the 11 of May 1641

30 Letter from Charles I to the House of Lords in favour of mercy for
the Earl of Strafford, 11 May 1641
Parliamentary Archives, HL/PO/JO/10/1/56A

31 Letter from Charles I to Prince Maurice, 25 June 1644 (one of the 'Naseby letters')
Parliamentary Archives, HL/PO/JO/10/1/183A

32 Engrossment made in 1651 of the official record of the trial of King Charles I
Parliamentary Archives, HL/PO/JO/10/14/11A

33 Death Warrant of King Charles I, 29 January 1649
Parliamentary Archives, HL/PO/JO/10/1/297A

Religion

The complexities of seventeenth century foreign policy and its relationship to the religious divides existing in Europe at that time is demonstrated by the letter from James I to Pope Gregory XV in 1622. The King asked the Pope to help end the war which had recently broken out between James' son-in-law, the Elector Palatine, and Spain. James did not wish, for various reasons, to be drawn into the dispute which was seen by many in England, however, as an opportunity to champion the Protestant cause.

In 1642 returns were made to Parliament of the names of those who had taken the protestation oath *'to maintain the true reformed Protestant religion'*. The collection of the returns, which was authorised by the Speaker of the House of Commons in January 1642, was motivated by a fear of Catholicism. Now a rich source for family historians, the returns survive for almost one third of English parishes; the return for Ramsey includes the names of Oliver Cromwell's uncle and cousin.

Following the restoration of Charles II in 1660 the Act of Uniformity was passed on 19 May 1662. The Act, which reflected the promotion of an Anglican religious settlement by the Government, provided for the introduction of a revised Book of Common Prayer from 24 August 1662. The manuscript copy of the Prayer Book held by the Parliamentary Archives was originally attached to the 1662 Act.

34 Draft letter from
James I to the Pope,
30 September 1622
Parliamentary Archives,
HL/PO/JO/10/1/22A

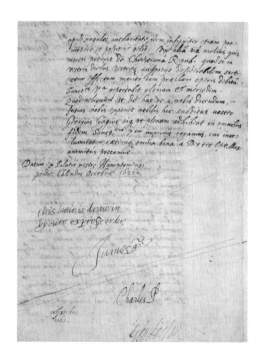

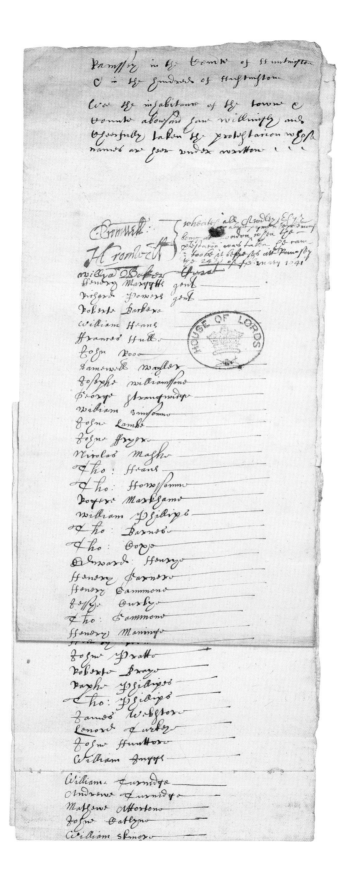

36 Book of Common
Prayer, 1636, with
annotations made in 1661
Parliamentary Archives,
HL/PO/LB/1/36/1

37 *An Act for the Uniformity
of Public Prayers and
Administration of Sacraments,
and other Rites and Ceremonies,
and for establishing the Form
of making, ordaining and
consecrating Bishops, Priests
and Deacons in the Church
of England* (the Act of
Uniformity), 14 Charles II,
c. 4, 1662
Parliamentary Archives,
HL/PO/PU/1/1662/14C2n3

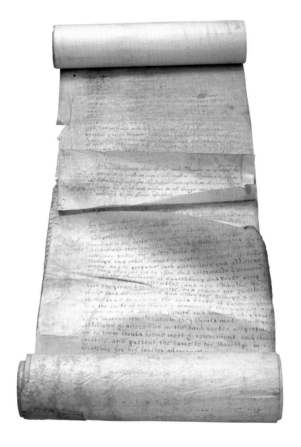

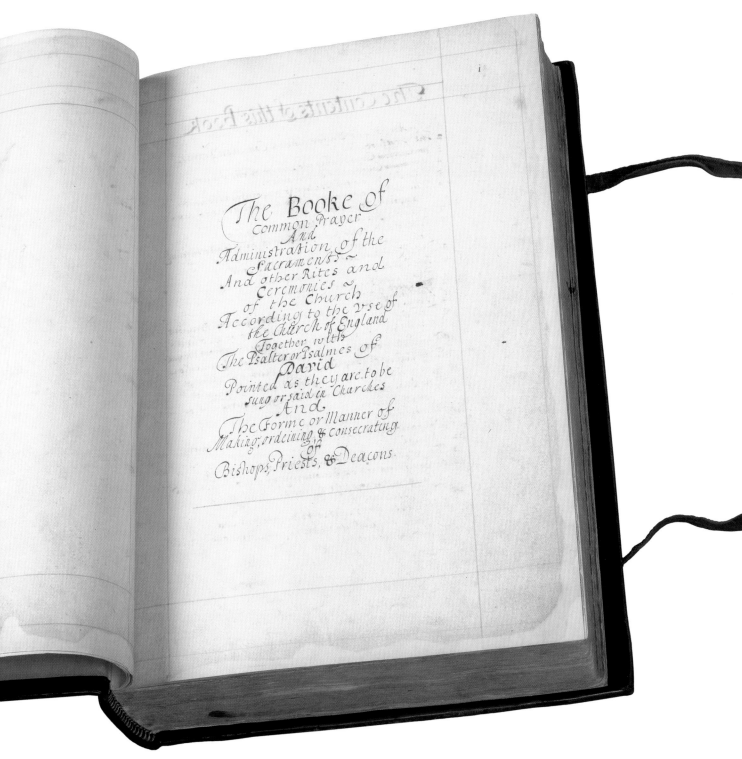

The Booke of
Common Prayer
And
Administration of the
Sacraments
And other Rites and
Ceremonies
of the Church
According to the vse of
the Church of England
Together with
The Psalter or Psalmes of
David
Pointed as they are to be
sung or said in Churches
And
The Forme or Manner of
Making, ordeining & consecrating
of
Bishops, Priests, & Deacons.

38 Manuscript copy of the 1662 Book of Common Prayer
Parliamentary Archives, HL/PO/LB/1/36/2

The Restoration

The Declaration of Breda, issued from Holland in April 1660 during Charles II's exile, set out his initial terms for the restoration of the Monarchy. The Declaration was a skilful political document, conciliatory but vague. It offered a general pardon and an amnesty for all offences committed during the Civil Wars, Commonwealth and Protectorate, with the exception of those committed by the regicides. It proposed that the terms of the Restoration settlement should be discussed by a freely elected parliament with Charles favouring liberty of conscience in religion and an equitable settlement of land disputes. This Declaration, with a wafer seal and Charles' signature, is the copy sent to the House of Lords; further copies went to the House of Commons, the Army, the Fleet and the City. Both Houses of Parliament unanimously voted for the Restoration. Charles wrote to the Speaker of the House of Lords, the Earl of Manchester, immediately on his return to England and it was read out in the House of Lords on 28 May 1660. It was dated '*in the Twelfth Year of Our Reign*' because Charles II counted his regnal years from the death of Charles I as if there had been no break.

A significant Act passed during the reign of Charles II was the Act designed to codify the ancient prerogative writ of Habeas Corpus. This prevented the unlawful detention of people by the authorities, giving courts the power to determine the legality of such imprisonment.

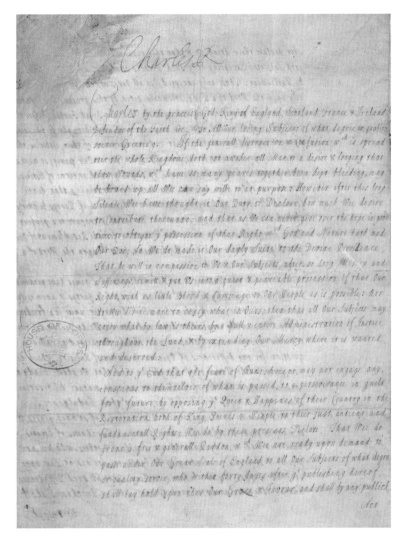

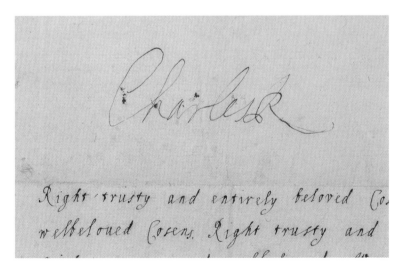

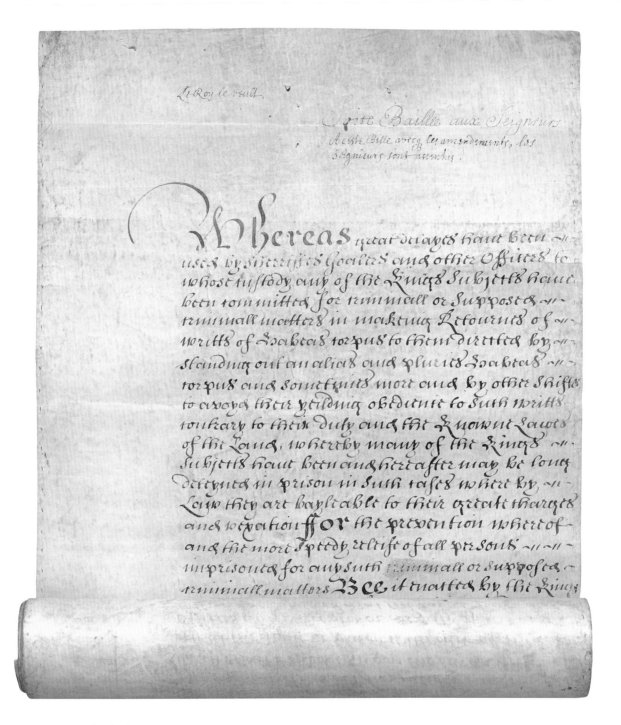

41 *An Act for the better securing the Liberty of the Subject, and for Prevention of Imprisonments beyond the Seas* (Habeas Corpus Act), 31 Charles II, c. 2, 1679

Parliamentary Archives, HL/PO/PU/1/1679/31C2n3

Dishes set before a King

Between 1189 and 1821 Westminster Hall was the traditional setting for coronation banquets. Over time the numbers attending these Royal feasts seems to have declined but, as is apparent from the image of the coronation banquet of James II on 23 April 1685, the concept of it being a spectacle had not diminished. Elaborate staging for onlookers was constructed in the Hall, whilst those participating in the event were served an enormous range of exotic dishes which included '*Oysters Pickled*', '*Hogs Tongues*', '*Three Dozen Glasses of Lemon Jelly*' and the spectacular '*square Pyramide, rising from Four large Dishes on the Angles, and Four lesser Dishes on the Sides, containing the several Fruits in season, and all manner of Sweetmeats*'.

42 *Coronation of James II* by Francis Sandford, 1687
Parliamentary Archives, LGC/8/1/5

The Glorious Revolution

Among the most important constitutional records held by the Parliamentary Archives are those relating to the Glorious Revolution of 1688–1689. This chain of events led to the Catholic King James II being replaced by his Protestant daughter Mary and her husband William, Prince of Orange.

Following the birth of a Catholic male heir to James II, William – with the encouragement of Parliament – landed at Brixham in Devon with 15,000 troops on 5 November 1688 to seize the throne. By December he had entered London and James fled the city (twice) and escaped to France, later complaining bitterly of his treatment in a letter which reached Parliament on 2 February 1689. The Commons' resolution states that James II *'having withdrawn himself out of this Kingdom has abdicated the Government and that the throne is thereby vacant'*. A Lords' amendment replaced the word *'abdicated'* with *'deserted'*.

The draft Declaration of Rights catalogued the means by which James had allegedly sought to subvert the Protestant religion of the country. It goes on to affirm the rights and liberties of the subject and that *'the Freedom of Speech and Debates, or Proceedings in Parliament, ought not to be impeached or questioned in any Court or Place out of Parliament'*. This principle is known as Parliamentary Privilege. The draft ends with the resolution that William and Mary be declared King and Queen of England. A bottle of ink was spilt over the draft by the Clerk during the debate on 12 February 1689 and the following day the engrossment (or fair copy) of the Declaration was read to William and Mary, the implication being that the offer was conditional on their acceptance of the terms it contained. They accepted.

A public proclamation was prepared by the House of Lords and agreed to by the Commons. It was published on 13 February 1689 at Charing Cross, the same day that the Declaration of Rights was read to William and Mary. In March 1689 James – now in Ireland – appealed to all his former subjects and promised liberty to the Church. Six copies of a beautifully printed proclamation were brought into Parliament and there debated. But it was too late. The engrossed Declaration served as the basis of the Act known as the Bill of Rights, passed in December 1689, which firmly established the principles of frequent parliaments, free elections, and freedom of speech within Parliament. It also prohibited the creation of standing armies without parliamentary consent and barred Catholics from the throne.

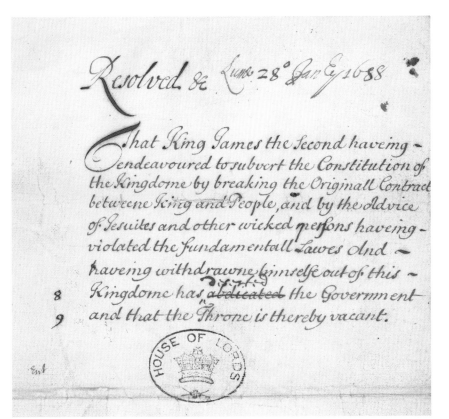

Resolved &c Luna 28° Jan Ey 1688

That King James the Second haveing
endeavoured to subvert the Constitution of
the Kingdome by breaking the Originall Contract
betweene King and People, and by the Advice
of Jesuites and other wicked persons haveing
violated the fundamentall Lawes And
haveing withdrawne himselfe out of this
Kingdome has abdicated the Government
and that the Throne is thereby vacant.

43 Commons' resolution
declaring that James II had
abdicated, and that the
throne is vacant,
28 January 1689
Parliamentary Archives,
HL/PO/JO/10/1/403A

James R

My Lords, wee think Ourselves bound in Conscience to doe all wee
can to open Our peoples eyes that they may see the true interest of the
Nation in this important Conjuncture, And therfor doe think fitt
to let you know, that finding wee Could no longer stay with safety
nor act with freedom in what Concerned Our people, And that it
was absolutely necessary for us to retire, wee left the reasons off
Our withdrawing under Our Own hand to be Communicated to you
and Our other Subjects in the following termes.

The world can not wonder at my withdrawing my self now this
second tyme. I might have expected somewhat better Vsage after
what I writ to the Prince of Orange by My Lord Feversham and
the Instructions I gave him; But instead of an Answer what
was I not to expect after the Vsage I receaved by the making
the said Earl a Prisonner against the Practice & law of
nations? The sending his Own guards at eleven at night to

44 Letter from James II to
Parliament, 2 February 1689
Parliamentary Archives,
HL/PO/JO/10/1/403C

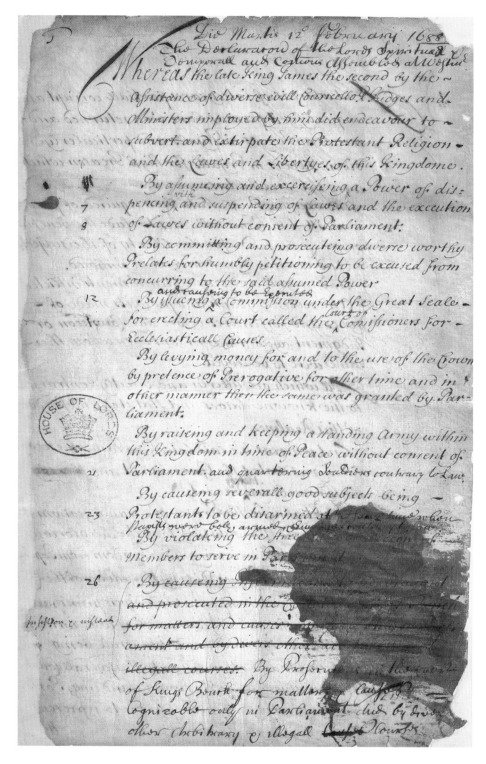

45 Draft Declaration of Rights, 12 February 1689

Parliamentary Archives, HL/PO/JO/10/1/403D

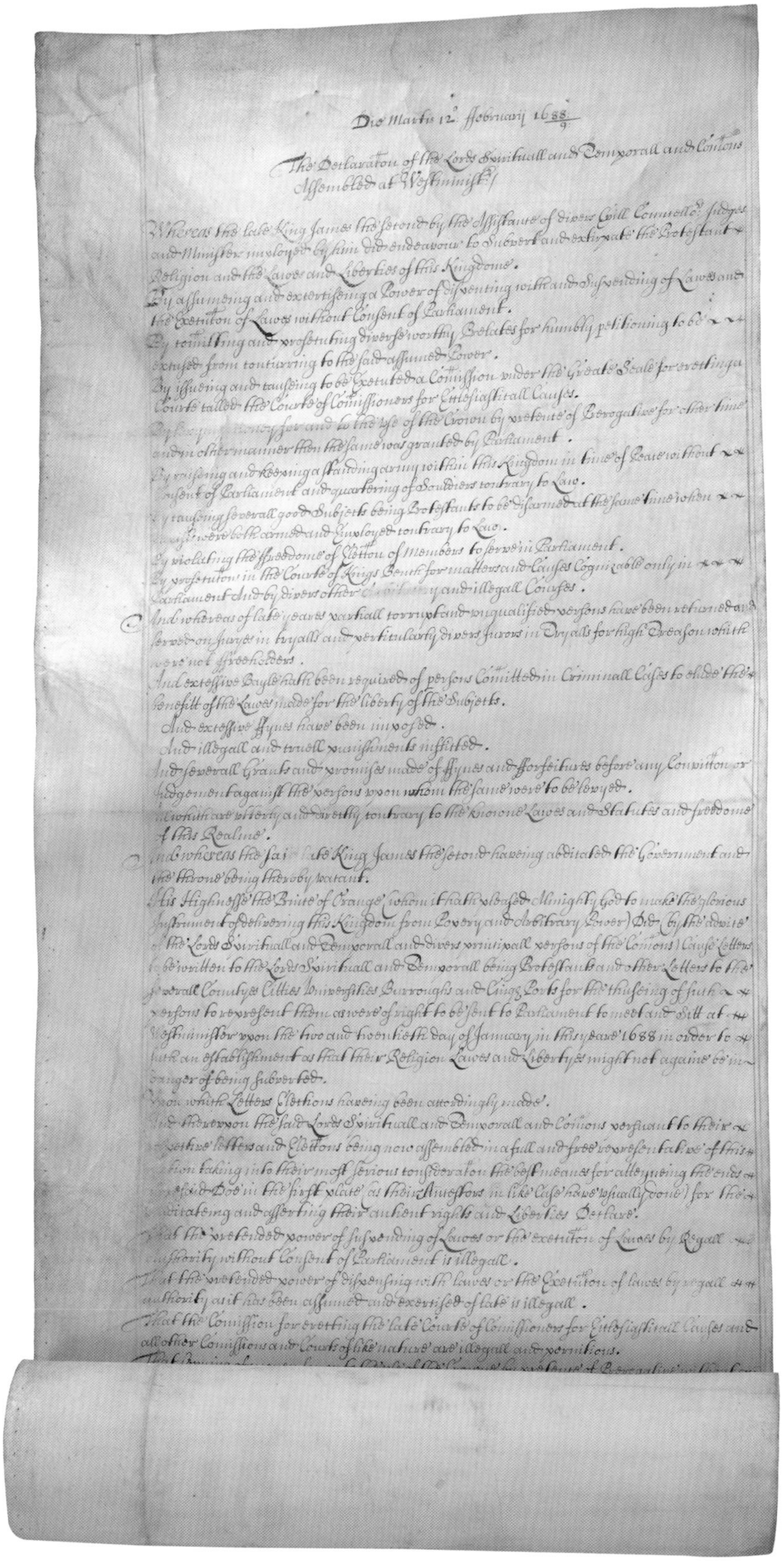

Die Martis 12° ffebruarij 1688/9

The Declaration of the Lords Spirituall and Temporall and Comons Assembled at Westminster

Whereas the late King James the second by the Assistance of diverse Evill Councellors Judges and Ministers imployed by him did endeavour to subvert and extirpate the Protestant Religion and the Lawes and Liberties of this Kingdome.

46 Engrossed Declaration of Rights, 12 February 1689
Parliamentary Archives, HL/PO/PU/1/1688/1W&Ms1n1

47 Proclamation for the Prince and Princess of Orange to be King and Queen, 12 February 1689
Parliamentary Archives, HL/PO/JO/10/1/403E

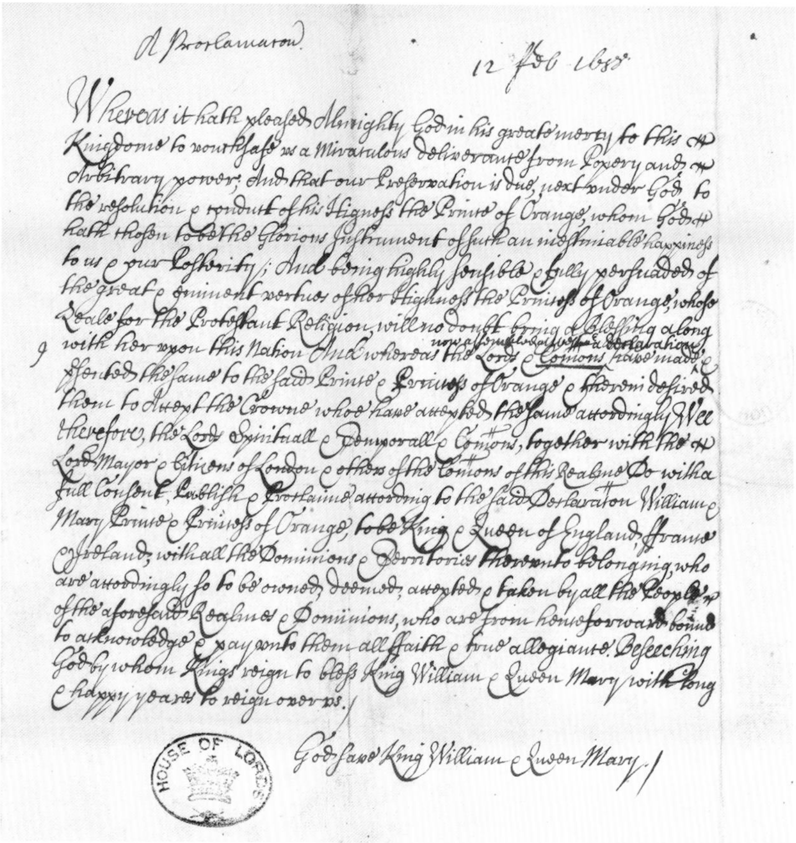
A Proclamation

12 Feb 1688

Whereas it hath pleased Almighty God in his great mercy to this Kingdome to vouchsafe us a Miraculous deliverance from Popery and Arbitrary power; And that our Preservation is due, next under God to the resolution & conduct of his Highness the Prince of Orange, whom God hath chosen to be the Glorious Instrument of such an inestimable happiness to us & our Posterity; And being highly sensible & fully persuaded of the great & eminent vertues of her Highness the Princess of Orange, whose Zeale for the Protestant Religion will no doubt bring a Blessing along with her upon this Nation And whereas the Lords & Comons now assembled at Westminster have made a Declaration & presented the same to the said Prince & Princess of Orange & therein desired them to accept the Crowne who have accepted the same accordingly Wee therefore, the Lords Spirituall & Temporall & Comons, together with the Lord Mayor & Citizens of London & others of the Comons of this Realme Do with a full Consent, Publish & Proclaime according to the said Declaration William & Mary Prince & Princess of Orange, to be King & Queen of England, France & Ireland, with all the Dominions & Territories thereunto belonging, who are accordingly so to be owned, deemed, accepted & taken by all the People of the aforesaid Realmes & Dominions, who are from henceforward bound to acknowledge & pay unto them all Faith & true allegiance. Beseeching God by whom Kings reign to bless King William & Queen Mary with long & happy yeares to reign over us.

God save King William & Queen Mary.

HOUSE OF LORDS

48 William of Orange's answer to the Declaration of Rights, 13 February 1689
Parliamentary Archives, HL/PO/JO/10/1/403F

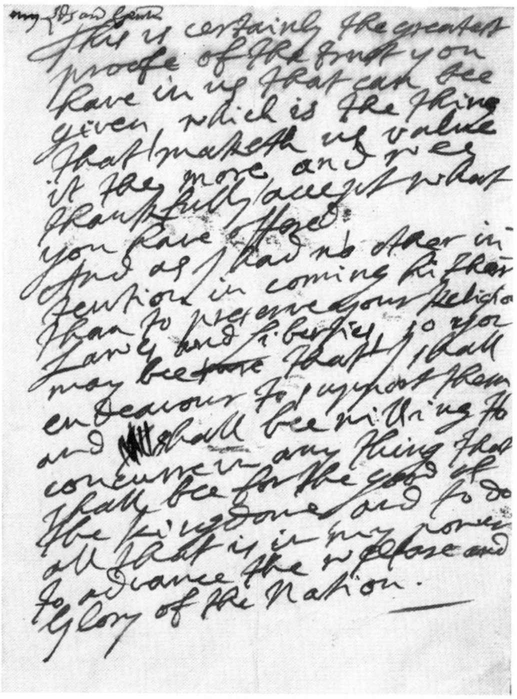
My Lords and Gentlemen

This is certainly the greatest proofe of the trust you have in us that can bee given which is the thing that maketh us value it the more and wee thankfully accept what you have offered. And as I had no other intention in coming hither than to preserve your Religion Lawes and liberties so you may bee sure that I shall endeavour to support them and shall bee willing to concurre in any thing that shall bee for the good of the kingdome and to do all that is in my power to advance the welfare and glory of the Nation.

49 Proclamation by James II
from Dublin, 1 April 1689
Parliamentary Archives,
HL/PO/JO/10/1/409A

50 *An Act declaring the Rights
and Liberties of the Subject,
and settling the Succession
of the Crown* (the Bill of
Rights), 1 William & Mary
Session 2, c. 2, 1689
Parliamentary Archives,
HL/PO/PU/1/1688/1W&Ms1n2

e Privy Seal, Signet, Cachet, Signet of the
isticiary Court, Quarter Seal and Seals of Court
oused in Scotland be continued; But that the said Seals
altered and adapted to the State of the Union as her
ajestie shall think fit. And the said Seals and all of them
the Keepers of them shall be subject to such Regulations
he Parliament of Great Britain shall hereafter make.

V. That all Laws and Statutes in either Kingdom
r as they are Contrary to or Inconsistent with the Terms
ese Articles or any of them shall from and after the
ion Cease and become Void. And shall be so Declared
by the respective Parliaments of the said Kingdoms.

In Testimony
Whereof the Commissioners for the
respective Kingdoms Impowered as
said have set their Hands and Seals to
Articles contained in this and the
ity seven foregoing pages at Westminster
Day and Year first above written.

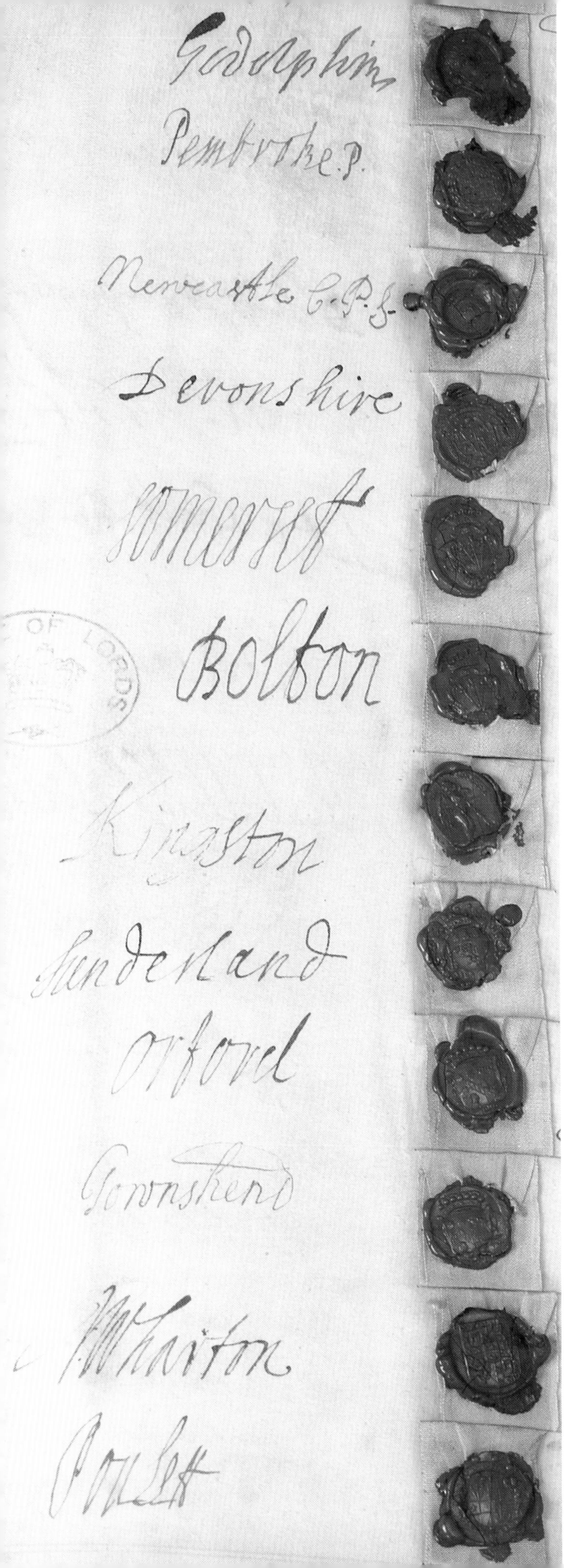

Godolphin
Pembroke.P.

Newcastle C.P.S.

Devonshire

Somerset

Bolton

Kingston

Sunderland

Orford

Townshend

Wharton

Poulet

The 18th
Century

Dynasty

The constitutional settlement of the Glorious Revolution included an Act that was passed more than ten years after the events of 1688–1689 which further strengthened Parliament and provided for Protestant succession to the throne. Passed in 1701, the Act of Settlement contained many articles that did not stand the test of time but included some that did, most notably the declaration that judges could only be removed by Parliament. In addition the Act stipulated that the throne was eventually to pass to the children of James I's daughter Elizabeth provided they *'join in communion with the Church of England'*. The Act led in 1714 to the Crown passing to the Elector of Hanover who became George I.

Despite the legislative basis for the succession, the threat posed by the Catholic Stuarts remained until the defeat of the Jacobite army by the Duke of Cumberland at Culloden in April 1746.

51 *An Act for the further Limitation of the Crown, and better securing the Rights and Liberties of the Subject* (the Act of Settlement), 12 & 13 William III, c. 2, 1701
Parliamentary Archives, HL/PO/PU/1/1700/13W3n2

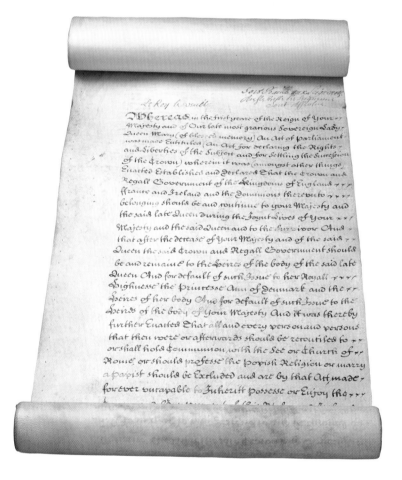

Inverness May y'e 7:th 1746

My Lord Chancellor. I could not possibly have received a more welcome and affecting proof of that distinguish'd Zeal & Loyalty, which the House of Lords have constantly shewn to his Majesty's Person & Government, than by their favourable acceptance of my Endeavours for the Publick Service; and I desire you would lay before the House my sincere acknowledgments for the Regard they have shewn me on this occasion.

The Resolution & Firmness express'd by Officer & Soldier in his Majesty's Army under my command, deserve the highest commendation; But the Guilt & Terror of that unhappy infatuated Multitude, who vainly hoped by unprovok'd Tumultuary arms, and a contemptible Foreign afistance, to shake an Establishment founded in the Hearts of his Majesty's Subjects, afforded us so easy a Victory,

52 Letter from the Duke of Cumberland following the Battle of Culloden, 15 May 1746
Parliamentary Archives, HL/PO/JO/10/6/531A

Monarch and Parliament

The Glorious Revolution changed the relationship between the Monarch and Parliament, tipping the balance of power away from the executive and towards the legislature. The Crown was now dependent on Parliament for financial support and Parliament assumed responsibility for raising money to finance public expenditure, including the costs of waging war.

This changed relationship is illustrated here by two documents. The significance of the first, the Militia of Scotland Bill, lies in the fact that it was the last bill to be refused Royal Assent by the Monarch. The Bill, which was intended to extend to Scotland a uniform approach to regulating the militia, was passed by both Houses and reached Royal Assent stage in the House of Lords on 11 March 1708, whereupon the Clerk of the Parliaments declared in the presence of Queen Anne '*La Reyne s'avisera*' ('The Queen will consider it').

The second document, a message from George III to the House of Lords in January 1793, was in effect a request for resources to counter the threat posed by France in the wake of the recent news of the execution of Louis XVI. The message was agreed to on 1 February and France declared war on Britain shortly afterwards.

53 Militia of Scotland
Bill, 1708
Parliamentary Archives,
HL/PO/JO/10/2/28A

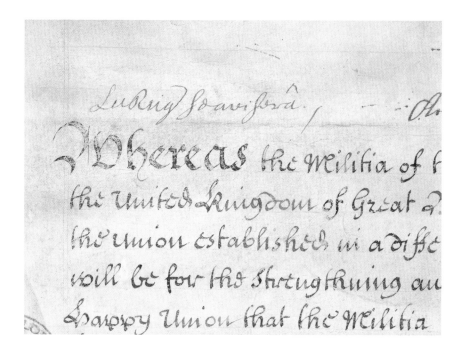

in consequence of the accounts
of the atrocious Act recently
perpetrated at Paris.

In the present Situation of
Affairs, His Majesty thinks
it indispensably necessary to
make a further Augmentation
of His Forces by Sea and Land,
and relies on the Known
affection and Zeal of the House
of Lords to concur in enabling
His Majesty to take the most
effectual Measures, in the
present important Conjuncture,
for maintaining the Security
and Rights of His own
Dominions, for supporting

His

His Allies, and for opposing
Views of aggrandisement
and ambition on the Part of
France, which would be at all
Times dangerous to the general
Interests of Europe, but are
peculiarly so when connected
with the Propagation of
Principles which lead to the
Violation of the most sacred
Duties, and are utterly
subversive of the Peace and
Order of all Civil Society.

54 Message from George III to the House of Lords, 28 January 1793
Parliamentary Archives, HL/PO/JO/10/7/929A

Union with Scotland

The failure of Elizabeth I to produce an heir, and the subsequent inheritance of the English Crown by James VI of Scotland in 1603, was not accompanied by a political union of the two countries which continued to have separate parliaments. Relations between the two countries were fraught and by the early 1700s there were fears that the constitutional settlement put in place after 1688 would be jeopardised by the Scots. Pressure from the English Parliament, however, and a realisation of the economic benefits to Scotland of a closer relationship led to the commencement of negotiations in 1706, which in turn led to the drawing up of the Articles of Union. Between January and March 1707 both Parliaments passed Acts incorporating the Articles and on 1 May 1707 the Union came into being, with the creation of the United Kingdom of Great Britain with a single parliament at Westminster, to which Scotland sent 45 MPs and 16 representative peers.

55 Articles of Union between England and Scotland, 22 July 1706
Parliamentary Archives, HL/PO/JO/10/6/106/2307

Wm Cooper. Es.

Godolphin

Pembroke. P.

Newcastle C.P.S.

Devonshire

Somerset

Bolton

Kingston

Sunderland

Orford

Townshend

Wharton

Poulet

Queensberry. C.P.S.

Mar~ S.

Loudon. S

Sutherland

Morton

Wemyss

Leven

Stair

Roseberie

Glasgow

Arch: Campbell

Dupplin

Ross

56 *An Act for an Union of the two Kingdoms of England and Scotland*, 6 Anne, c. 11, 1707
Parliamentary Archives, HL/PO/PU/1/1706/5&6An14

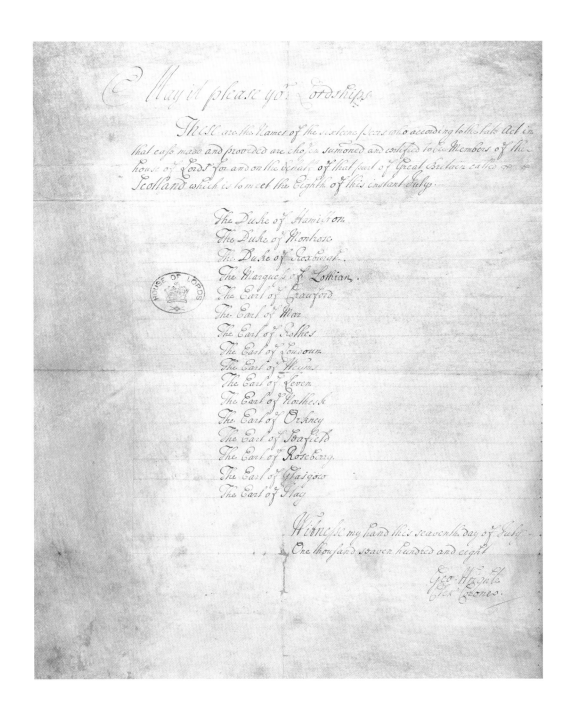

57 Return of Scottish representative peers, 7 July 1708

Parliamentary Archives, HL/PO/JO/10/6/150A

Citizenship

Until 1844 a foreign-born individual could only become a British subject by means of an Act of Parliament. The process, which was known as naturalisation, was often undertaken by means of a private Act which named a specific person. In addition to taking the Oaths of Supremacy and Allegiance in both Houses of Parliament the individual concerned had to produce a certificate testifying that Holy Communion according to the Church of England had been received. One such individual was the composer George Frideric Handel who was born in Halle, Saxony, in 1685. By 1712 Handel had settled permanently in England but he was not naturalised by Act of Parliament until 1727.

Although Parliament could define citizenship by passing an Act, some individuals challenged parliamentary authority in order to achieve new rights for ordinary citizens. This was true of John Wilkes who, whilst an MP in the early 1760s, published attacks on the Government for which he was arrested and expelled from the House of Commons. In 1768 Wilkes, who had fled to France in 1763, was elected MP for Middlesex but shortly afterwards was imprisoned for his previous offences, in relation to which he petitioned the House of Lords in December 1768. Although he was expelled from the House of Commons in February 1769, Wilkes was subsequently elected for Middlesex three times between February and April that year.

58 *An Act for naturalizing Louis Sechehaye, George Frideric [Frederick] Handel, Anthony Fursteneau and Michael Schlegel,* 13 George I, c. 2, 1727
Parliamentary Archives, HL/PO/PB/1/1726/13G1n3

That your Petitioner is advised it will be necessary for him to Attend this Hon'ble house on the Arguing the said Errors to be ready to Instruct his Councel therein (if Occasion should require)

Your Petitioner therefore most Humbly prays your Lordships to Order the Marshal of the Kings Bench Prison to bring your Petitioner on Wednesday next to the Bar of this Honourable house that he may be present to Instruct his Councel (if Occasion Should require) upon the Arguing the said Errors

And your Petitioner shall ever pray

John Wilkes

59 Petition of John Wilkes to the House of Lords, 19 December 1768
Parliamentary Archives, HL/PO/JO/10/7/293B

The Colonies

The change in the relationship between Britain and her American colonies during the eighteenth century is reflected in documents in the Parliamentary Archives. The petition from the Penn family on behalf of the people of Pennsylvania in 1731 against a bill then before the House of Lords which was prejudicial to their interests, demonstrates the legislative and parliamentary ties which were still in place, whereas the Act passed by Parliament in 1765, commonly known as the Stamp Act, proved to be a watershed in relations between Britain and America. The Act imposed taxes on goods and services, including legal documents and appointments to public offices, in order to pay for military expenses in America and caused widespread protest and questioning of Parliament's right to tax the colonies which were not represented at Westminster. The strength of feeling is apparent from the copy of the *New-York Gazette* of December 1765 which was amongst a batch of papers laid before the House of Lords in February 1766. A month later the Stamp Act was repealed but relations with America were never the same. Following the Boston Tea Party of December 1773, Parliament passed a series of Acts in 1774 designed to impose British authority on Massachusetts. The Acts, which became known as the Intolerable Acts, were accompanied by the Quebec Act which attempted to provide a settlement for the British acquisition of French Canada but which provoked anger in the American colonies. The petition to the House of Lords of 11 May 1774 against the Intolerable Acts was signed by, among others, Benjamin Franklin, the radical colonial politician. The outbreak of fighting at Lexington in 1775 symbolised the breakdown of the colonial relationship and, on 4 July the following year, the 13 colonies declared themselves independent.

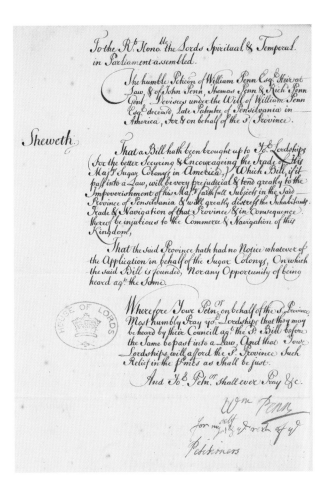

62 *The New-York Gazette*; or *The Weekly Post-Boy*, Thursday, December 19, 1765, laid before the House of Lords on 10 February 1766

Parliamentary Archives, HL/PO/JO/10/7/210A

THURSDAY, *December* 19, 1765.   NUMB. 1198.

THE

NEW-YORK GAZETTE;

OR THE

WEEKLY POST-BOY.

With the freſheſt Advices Foreign and Domeſtick.

The united Voice of all His Majeſty's *free* and *loyal* Subjects in
AMERICA,
LIBERTY and PROPERTY, and NO STAMPS.

The PRINTER *to the* PUBLICK.

WHEREAS it manifeſtly appears to be the unanimous Sentiment of all his Majeſty's free and loyal Subjects throughout all his extenſive Dominions in America, that the STAMP ACT is not legally binding upon them, nor in Force in any Part of the ſaid Dominions, nor could be put in Execution without deſtroying their Rights as Engliſhmen, and that Conſtitution by which his Majeſty holds his Title to the Crown of Great-Britain, and the Dominions thereunto belonging in America, &c. And whereas it alſo appears, that the Execution of the ſaid Act is impracticable, even if any Perſon in America could be found inclinable to admit of it—ſince there is no Officer in America qualified to be a Diſtributor of the Stamps, nor any Perſon that can either deliver them, or receive, or apply for them without certain Deſtruction to his Perſon and Property from the general Reſentment of his Countrymen—nor any Perſon in any public Office, who can refuſe or delay the Execution of the ordinary Buſineſs belonging to it, under Pretence of the Want of Stamps, required by the ſaid Act, or Fear of the Penalties mentioned in it; nor require, nor pay any Obedience to it, without the like Danger to his Perſon and Effects.—Therefore, for all theſe and other Conſiderations, the Printer of this Paper has concluded to continue his weekly Publications, as uſual, upon unſtamped Paper; which, as they have been hitherto, he intends ever ſhall be, ſacred to Liberty,—and, conſequently, to Virtue, and Religion, the Good of his Country and Mankind.—And he hopes that Country which he has earneſtly endeavoured to ſerve, and thoſe conſtitutional Laws, which he has ever obeyed and endeavoured to maintain, as a faithful Subject to his Majeſty, will protect him in any Hazards to which he is expoſed by his difficult Situation.

To His Excellency Sir HENRY MOORE, Baronet, &c.

May it pleaſe your Excellency,

THE Miniſter and Church Wardens of the ancient Lutheran Church in New-York, humbly beg Leave to congratulate Your Excellency upon Your Appointment to the Government of this Province; and upon Your ſafe Arrival here, with Your Lady and Family, after a hazardous and fatiguing long Voyage.

We do, with the greateſt Gratitude, acknowledge His Moſt Gracious Majeſty's paternal Care and Affection, in appointing over Us, a Gentleman of diſtinguiſhed Character and Abilities, which affords us ſufficient Hope, of being happy under Your Excellency's Adminiſtration.

Our Church, from it's firſt Foundation, hath happily enjoyed under that glorious Britiſh Conſtitution, an undiſturbed Exerciſe of our Religious Rights and Privileges: a Continuance whereof, we humbly Hope for, under Your Excellency's Government.

A   That

63 Petition against the Intolerable Acts, 11 May 1774

Parliamentary Archives, HL/PO/JO/10/3/265B

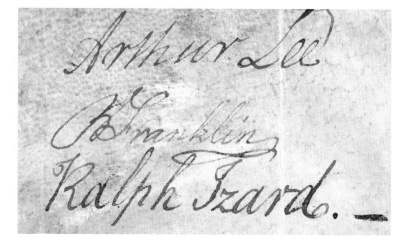

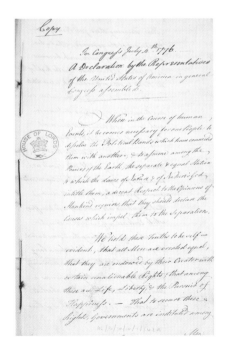

64 *An Act for making more effectual Provision for the Government of the Province of Quebec in North America,* 14 George III, c. 83, 1774
Parliamentary Archives, HL/PO/PU/1/1774/14G3n226

65 Copy of the American Declaration of Independence of 4 July 1776, laid before the House of Lords on 20 January 1778
Parliamentary Archives, HL/PO/JO/10/7/542A

The Slave Trade

By the middle of the eighteenth century European demand for sugar and tobacco had led to the development of extensive plantations in the Americas, particularly the West Indies. These plantations were worked by enslaved Africans who, having been exchanged for European goods on the West African coast, were shipped across the Atlantic on slave ships.

The letter supporting the Governor of Cape Coast Castle was amongst several papers presented to Parliament in 1751. It is an astonishing document, since it is signed (marked) by Africans working at Cape Coast Castle in 1749 who pleaded that an official, who had treated them fairly, should not be dismissed. Cape Coast Castle was a fort on the west coast of Africa that had been built by the Royal Africa Company which participated in the trade in enslaved Africans.

In the late eighteenth century Paliament passed legislation which regulated the British slave trade. In compliance with this legislation the captains of slave ships detailed on a certificate the number of individuals they carried during a voyage.

66 Letter in support of the Governor of Cape Coast Castle, 10 February 1749
Parliamentary Archives, HL/PO/JO/10/7/8

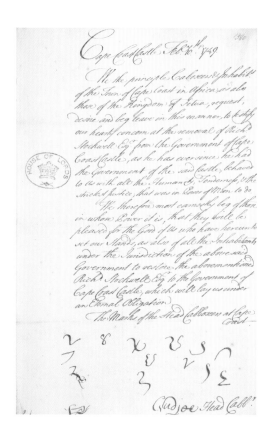

SAINT VINCENT.

IN Pursuance of an Act made and passed in the Thirty-first Year of his present Majesty, intitled, " An Act to continue for a limited Time and to amend an Act made in the last Session of Parliament, intitled, ' An Act to amend and continue, for a limited Time, several Acts of Parliament for regulating the shipping and carrying Slaves in *British* Vessels from the Coast of *Africa*."

I, *Andrew Chester* Master of the Ship or Vessel called the *Express* of *London* laden with Slaves from the Coast of *Africa*, do deliver the underwritten exact and true Account of the greatest Number of Slaves that were or have been in or on Board the said Ship or Vessel at any one Time before, when, or after such Ship or Vessel quitted or departed from the Coast of *Africa*, viz. from the *twenty third* Day of *February* 1793 to the *Fourth* Day of *October* 179*3. one hundred & twenty Eight* Slaves, whereof —— *110* —— did exceed the Height of Four Feet Four Inches.

The *Express* cleared out from *London* the *20th* Day of *December* 179*2* and arrived on the Coast the *twenty third Feby 1793* the whole Number of Slaves taken on Board on the Coast, were *& three Eighty one* —— Males, and *forty four* —— Females, above Four Feet Four Inches, and *fourteen* Males and *eight* —— Females under Four Feet Four Inches.

Total, - - - - - - *147*
Deduct *16* Males and *5* Females, *21*
delivered on board *Shore at diff. times*
126
above 4 = 4 *1*
one Males and Females deceased; *125*

Arrived at *St. Vincent*, the *fourth* Day of *October* 1793 *64* Males and *30* Females exceeding Four Feet Four Inches, and *14* Males and *8* Females under Four Feet Four Inches.

Total *125*

128 Slaves were the greatest Number on board at any one Time, whereof *71* being Male Slaves, did exceed the Height of Four Feet Four Inches.

Witness my Hand, this *7th* Day of *October 1793*

Andw Chester

67 Certificate signed by a slave ship captain, 7 October 1793
Parliamentary Archives, HL/PO/JO/10/7/982A

India

Below left:

68 Pass for Joseph Gurney, shorthand reporter, to attend the trial of Warren Hastings, 1789
Parliamentary Archives, HL/PO/LB/1/55

Below right:

69 Petition from Warren Hastings for the close of his trial, 18 April 1793
Parliamentary Archives, HL/PO/JO/10/7/944A

The growth in British influence in India during the eighteenth century was driven, to a large extent, by individuals such as Robert Clive and Warren Hastings. The activities of both men were scrutinised by Parliament but, of the two, it was Hastings who received the most intense and prolonged attention. Following his return to England from India in 1785 Hastings faced charges brought by Edmund Burke relating to his conduct there and, on 10 May 1787, he was impeached on charges which included allegations of corruption.

Hastings' trial took place in Westminster Hall where tiered seating was erected on both sides, thereby ensuring that the event became a public spectacle attracting enormous crowds. Beginning in 1788, the trial lasted until 1795 when Hastings was found not guilty of the charges.

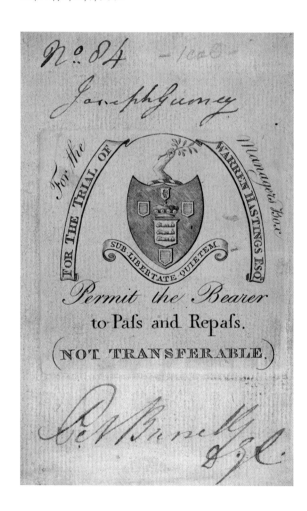

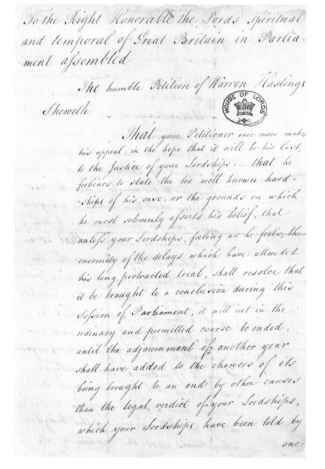

70 Shorthand notebook for the trial of Warren Hastings, 17 May 1793

Parliamentary Archives, GUR/80

Lines of Descent

In accordance with a Standing Order of the House of Lords of 11 May 1767 peers taking up their seat in the House were required to produce a pedigree. These consisted of family trees and an illuminated coat of arms. The Standing Order was repealed in 1802.

John Montagu succeeded his father as the 5th Earl of Sandwich in 1792. He took his seat in the House of Lords on 9 May 1792 when he delivered his pedigree which was verified by the Committee for Privileges in 1793.

71 Pedigree of the Earl of Sandwich, 1792
Parliamentary Archives, HL/PO/JO/22/1/4

JOHN MONTAGU Earl *of SANDWICH*.

John Montagu *Earl of Sandwich Viscount Hinchingbrook & Baron Montagu of S.t Neots; born 4. Nov.r 1718. died at his House in Hertford Street May 3.ur 30. April 1792 buried at Barnwell* — Dorothy *Daughter of Charles Fane Viscount Fane of the Kingdom of Ireland married at S.t James's Westminster 14. March 1740.41. living 1792.*

John Montagu *first Son born 18 Dec.r 1742, buried at S.t George's Hanover Square 8 Jan.y following*

Elizabeth *only surviving Daur & Heir of George Montagu-Dunk Earl of Halifax; marr: at S.t Margarets Westminster 8. Mar:1766 died 1 July 1768 & buried at Barnwell near Oundle in the County of Northampton.* — John Montagu *only surviving Son now Earl of Sandwich. Viscount Hinchingbrook & Baron Montagu of S.t Neots; born in the Parish of S.t George Hanover Square 26 Jan.y & bapt.d 22.d Feb.y 1743.4.*

Mary *eldest daur of Harry Paulet Duke of Bolton, married at Hackwood Co. Hants 25 April 1772; died 31 Mar.r 1779 buried at Barnwell aforesaid*

Edward Montagu *3.d Son born 30 June 1745, died 2. Nov.r 1752.*

William-Augustus Montagu *4.th Son born 1752 died unmarried at Lisbon in Jan.y 1776*

Mary *one daur born 23 of Feb.y 1748 died unmar:d June 176*

John-George Montagu *first Son born in the Parish of Marybone 3 Apr. & bap.d 4. May 1767, died without Issue Nov.r 1790 buried at Barnwell.* — Dorothy-Charlotte *only Child of Stephen Beckingham of Portman Square Esq.r & of Bourn Place in Kent. Living a Widow*

Carolina-Maria *died unmarried bur. at Marybone 5 July 1782.*

George Montagu *born in the Parish of Marybone 4 Feb.y & bapt.d 5 March 1773.*

Mary *born in the Parish of Marybone 1 Jan.y & bapt.d 27 Feb.y 1774.*

Francis-Charles Henrietta-Susanna *both died Infants.*

POST TOT NAUFRAGIA PORTUM

Warming the House

The great architect Sir John Soane was appointed Clerk of the Works to St James's Palace and the Houses of Parliament in 1791. In 1794 he was commissioned to provide a better ventilation scheme for the Lords' Chamber, on the back of which he ambitiously prepared designs for remodelling much of the Palace of Westminster. His plans were considered by a committee of the House, and he continued to develop them until 1798 when they were dropped in favour of those by his arch-rival James Wyatt, the Surveyor-General of Works, on the orders of George III. This cross-section of his proposed heating system shows the cellar of the House of Lords which Guy Fawkes had tried to blow up in 1605. In 1800 the Lords moved from this medieval building to a more spacious one, also dating from the thirteenth century, in order that Irish peers could be accommodated after the Act of Union. Soane's grand designs for both Houses continued to be thwarted by a variety of means until the 1820s, when he was finally able to build a grand neo-classical suite of rooms for the Lords. Ironically, that included the demolition of the ancient building shown here.

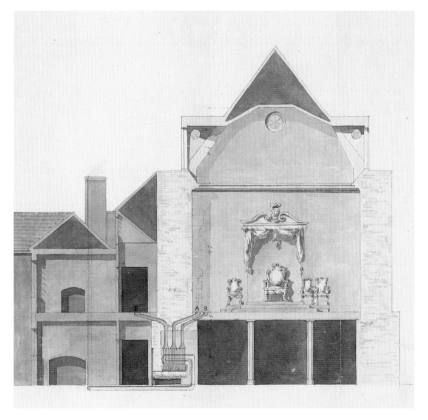

72 Sir John Soane's plan for warming and ventilating the House of Lords, 1794
Parliamentary Archives, HL/PO/JO/10/7/980A

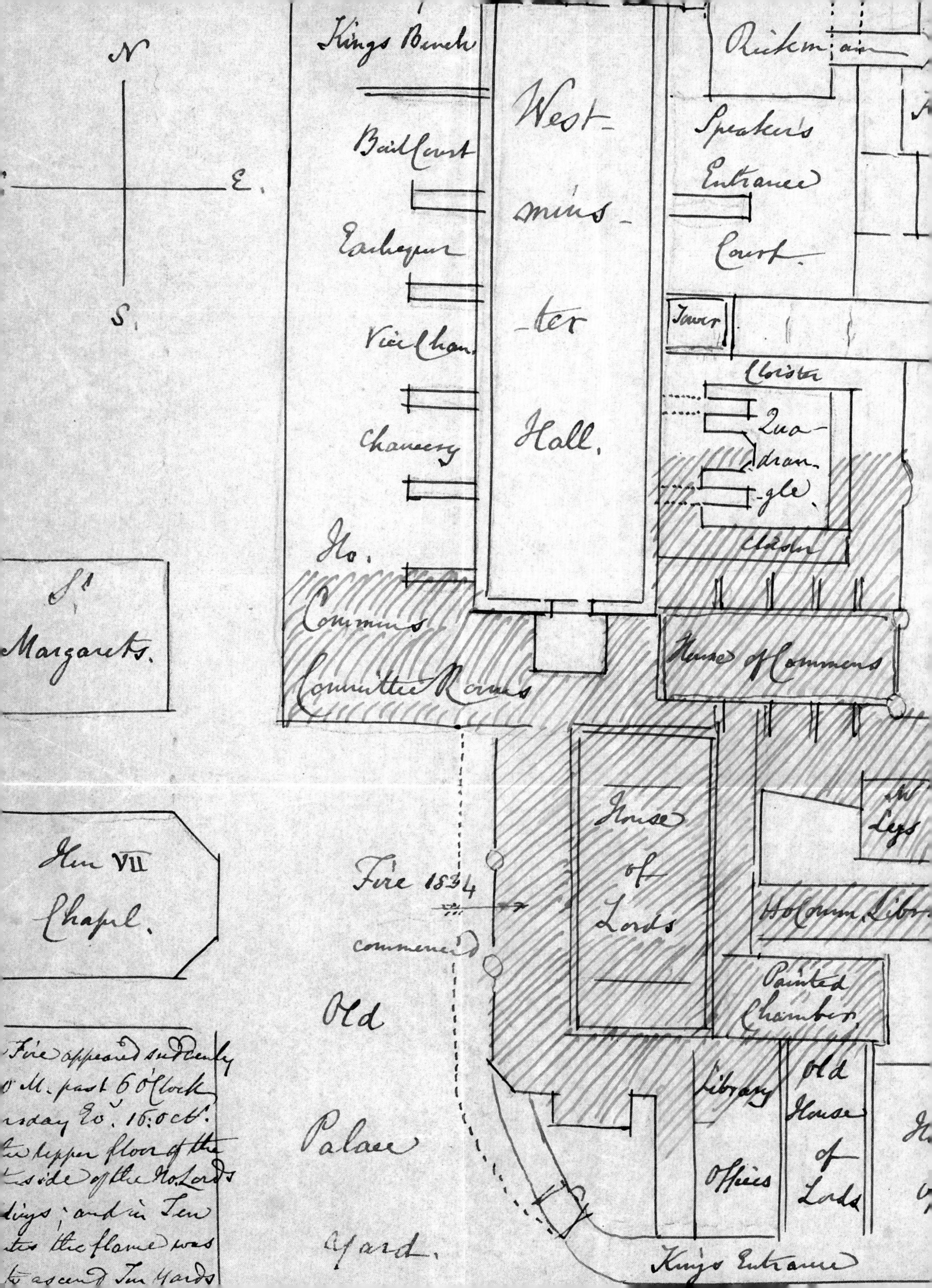

N

E.

S.

Kings Bench

Bail Court

Exchequer

Vice Chan.

Chancery

Ho.
of
Commons
Committee Rooms

West-
mins-
-ter

Hall.

Rickman

Speaker's
Entrance

Court.

Tower

Cloister

Qua-
dran-
-gle.

Cloister

House of Commons

St
Margaret's.

Hen VII
Chapel.

Fire 1834

commenced

Old

Palace

Yard.

House
of
Lords

Ho Comm Library

Painted
Chamber

Library

Offices

Old
House
of
Lords

Ho
Legs

Kings Entrance

Fire appeared suddenly
0 M. past 6 O'clock
rsday 20. 16. Oct.
upper floor of the
side of the Ho Lords
dings; and in Ten
the flame was
ascend Ten Yards

The 19th Century

Union with Ireland

The possibility of a union between Great Britain and Ireland had been discussed since the mid-seventeenth century but the rebellion of 1798 threw the issue into focus and, combined with a threat of French invasion, led the British Government to consider it seriously. Despite initial Irish opposition, the Dublin and Westminster Parliaments both passed Acts which created the United Kingdom of Great Britain and Ireland. Under the terms of the Union, which came into effect on 1 January 1801, the Irish Parliament was abolished; Ireland was given 100 MPs at Westminster whilst Irish peers were represented in the House of Lords by 28 of their number who served for life. Four Church of Ireland bishops also joined the Lords by rotation.

73 *An Act for the Union of Great Britain and Ireland,* 39&40 George III, c. 67, 1800

Parliamentary Archives, HL/PO/PU/1/1800/39&40G3n241

The Upper House

In early parliaments Members of the House of Lords were occasionally expected to swear an oath of allegiance and, since the seventeenth century, this procedure has been defined and amended by legislation for Members of both Houses. In the early nineteenth century peers were required, before taking part in the proceedings of the House, to take oaths of supremacy and allegiance and to sign the Test Roll. This process was repeated for each parliament.

By the late seventeenth century claims to peerages were referred to the House of Lords and from 1621 such claims were heard by the Committee for Privileges. The Committee considered evidence submitted by claimants and the nature of this could vary dramatically. In 1845 James Tracy submitted fragments of a tombstone as evidence in support of his claim to be Viscount Tracy of Rathcoole. The Tracy peerage, which had been declared extinct in 1797, was an Irish title and would only have given Tracy a seat in the House of Lords under the terms of the Union with Ireland Act of 1800 which provided for 28 elected Irish peers. The Committee for Privileges considered the evidence in 1847 when a witness testified that the fragments were forgeries. Before the Committee could reach a decision, Tracy died. In contrast, the evidence submitted by Viscount Gort in 1818 in support of his claim to vote at elections of Irish peers consisted of the colourful Letters Patent relating to the creation of his uncle as Baron Kiltarton of Gort in 1810.

74 Test Roll, House of Lords, 1801, with the signature of Horatio, Lord Nelson
Parliamentary Archives, HL/PO/JO/8/71A

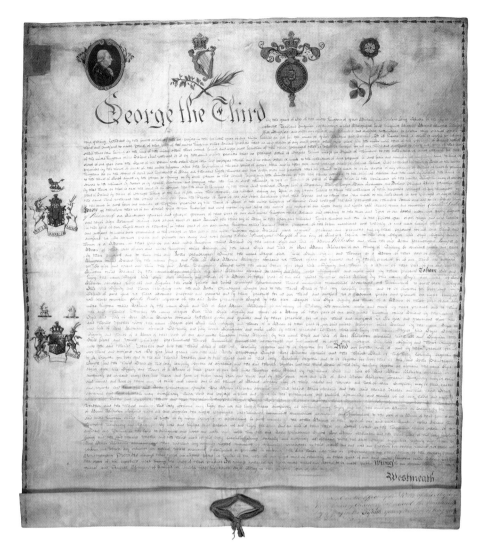

75 Letters Patent of Baron Kiltarton
of Gort, 18 May 1810, submitted
to the House of Lords Committee
for Privileges, 1818
Parliamentary Archives,
HL/PO/JO/10/3/294A

76 Tombstone fragment submitted to the House of Lords Committee
for Privileges by James Tracy, 1845
Parliamentary Archives, HL/PO/DC/CP/3/105A

Private Lives

Divorce by legal process only became possible after the Matrimonial Causes Act of 1857. Before that date the only way to get a full divorce which allowed re-marriage was to obtain an Act of Parliament by proving adultery or life-threatening cruelty. In the House of Lords divorce bills were usually considered by a committee of the whole House and evidence was given there by witnesses. The evidence can give large amounts of personal information about the people involved, as maids, butlers and coachmen were called alongside family members to testify about the state of the marriage.

The roll pictured is the Act for the Addison-Campbell divorce of 1801, together with other documents relating to the same case. This is a significant case as it was the first divorce to be obtained by a woman. Jane Campbell managed to divorce her husband, Edward Addison, on the grounds of incestuous adultery with her sister, Jessy Campbell. She also obtained custody of their children, which was unusual for a woman in this period. Evidence was given by Jessy Campbell's maid that Mr Addison had frequently visited her mistress in his dressing gown and slippers 'About an Hour or an Hour and an Half after she had been Bed'.

Opposite:

77 An Act to dissolve the Marriage of Jane Campbell with Edward Addison her now Husband, on account of his incestuous Adultery with the Sister of the said Jane Campbell, and to enable the said Jane Campbell to marry again; and for other purposes therein mentioned, 41 George III, c. 102, 1801
Parliamentary Archives, HL/PO/PB/1/1801/41G3n287

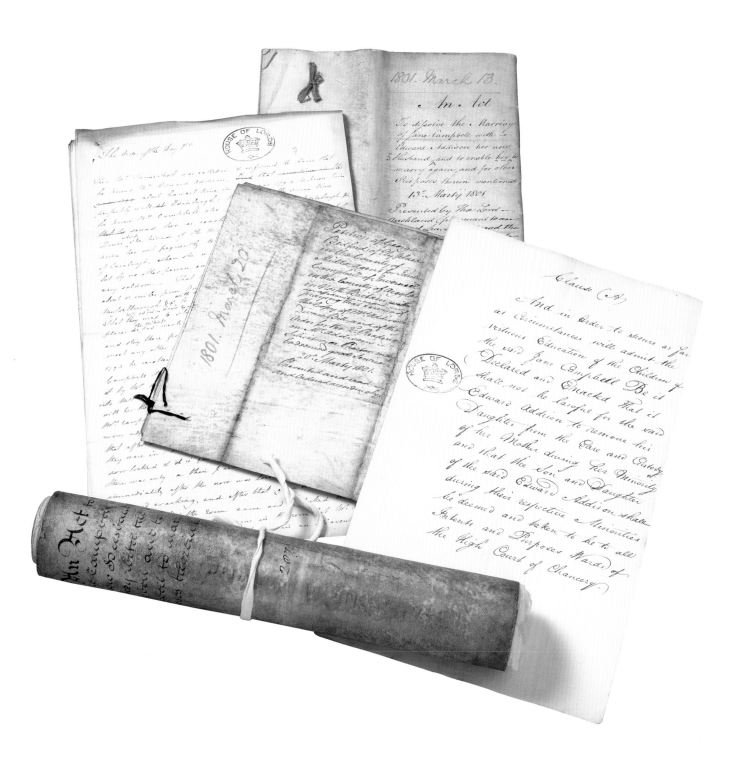

Changing the Landscape

Parliament has played a central part in changes to the landscape, mainly through the passing of Acts that have authorised the construction of roads, canals, railways and other works. The period when this was at its height was the nineteenth century when, in particular, the number of Acts for building railways reached a peak. From 1794 it was a requirement for promoters of such bills to deposit in Parliament plans and associated documents before the bill in question began its progress through both Houses.

Taken as a whole, these records help document the history of transport over several centuries. The Croydon to Reigate railway, for example, was an extension to the Surrey Iron Railway, the world's first statutorily incorporated public railway. The proposed line was designed by William Jessop and used horses to haul wagons. It was never finished and closed in 1846. The letter and estimate of expense from the railway engineer George Stephenson is typical of the material that was deposited with plans for railways and such items give a valuable insight into the planning of such an undertaking.

The plans themselves are often colourful and full of detail of the landscape and environment; as such they constitute a valuable source for local and family historians. The plan drawn up by the civil engineer Ralph Dodd for the proposed South London Waterworks in 1804 clearly shows details of streets and properties in South London, including the Kennington Oval and the Vauxhall Pleasure Gardens.

In addition to the plans, the Parliamentary Archives holds a large quantity of evidence taken from individuals in relation to bills which were opposed. Many of the witnesses giving such evidence were well-known, such as the engineer Isambard Kingdom Brunel, whilst others were ordinary members of the public who would be affected by the scheme in question.

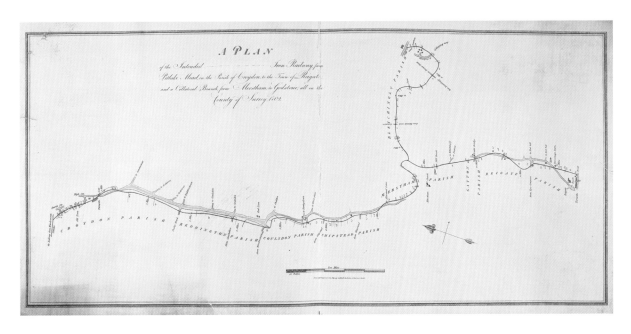

78 Plan of a railway from Croydon to Reigate with a branch from Merstham to Godstone, Surrey, 1802
Parliamentary Archives, HL/PO/PB/3/plan8

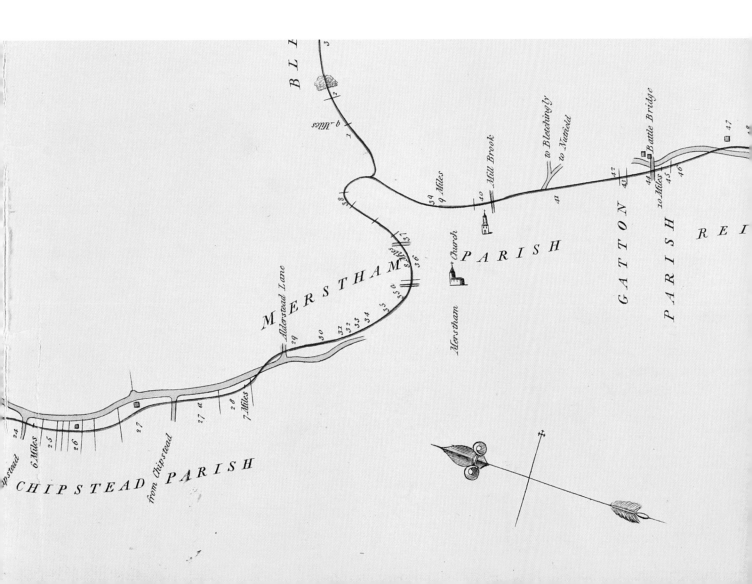

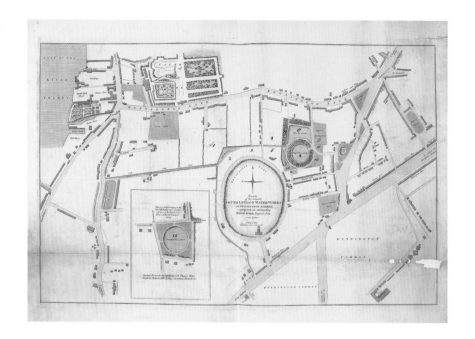

79 Plan of proposed South
London Waterworks at
Kennington, Surrey, 1804
Parliamentary Archives,
HL/PO/PB/3/plan8

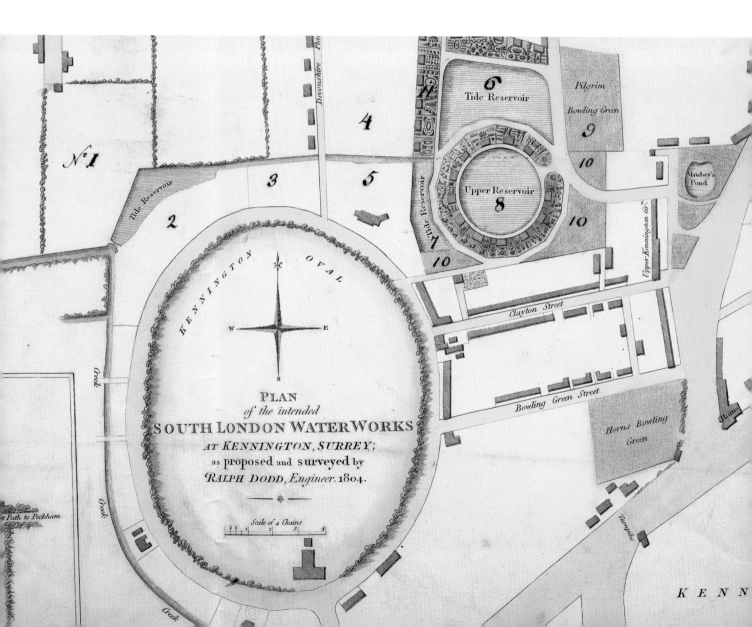

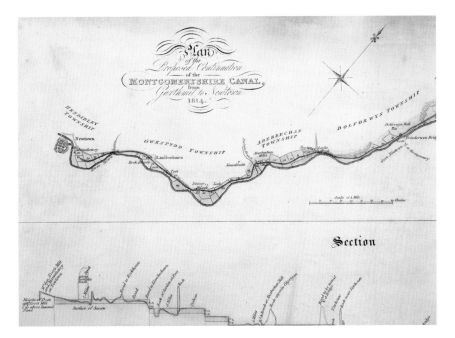

Left:

80 Plan of an extension
to the Montgomeryshire
Canal from Garthmyl
to Newtown, 1814
Parliamentary Archives,
HL/PO/PB/3/plan19

Below:

81 Chart of Port Nessock
Bay and plan of a proposed
harbour, 1818
Parliamentary Archives,
HL/PO/PB/3/plan23

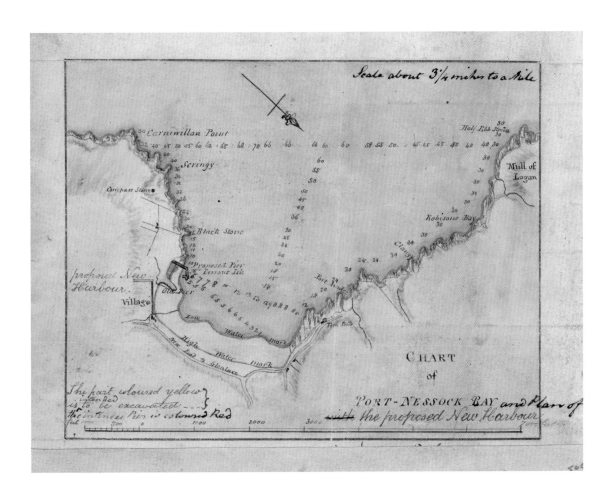

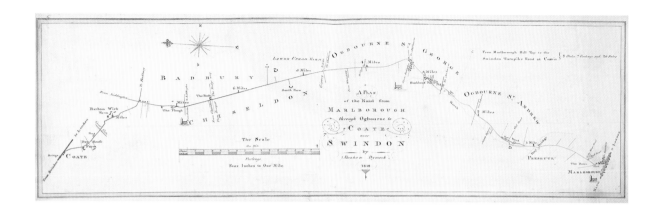

82 Plan of a road from Marlborough to Coate, near Swindon, Wiltshire, 1818
Parliamentary Archives, HL/PO/PB/3/plan26

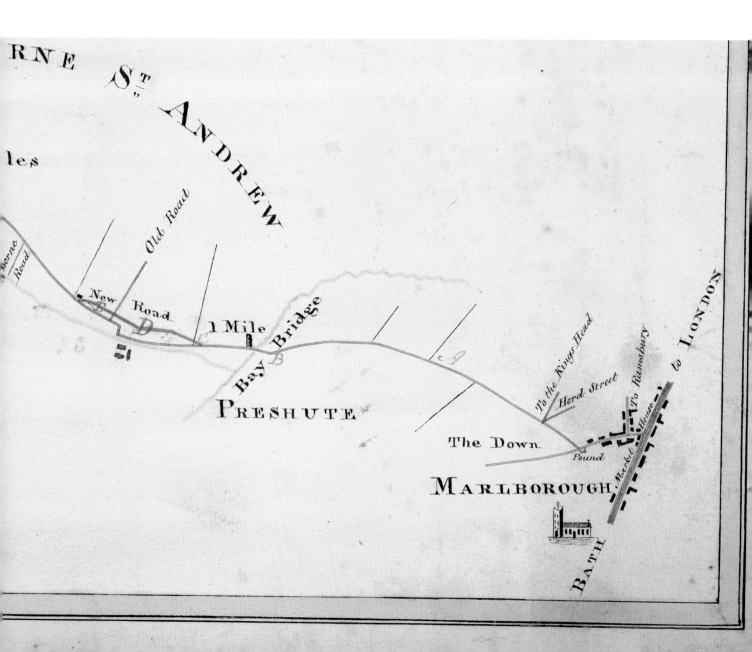

83 Letter and estimate of expense from George Stephenson relating to an extension to the Stockton and Darlington Railway, 18 September 1827
Parliamentary Archives, HL/PO/PB/3/plan61a

84 Evidence given by Isambard Kingdom Brunel on the South Devon Railway Bill, 1846
Parliamentary Archives, HC/CL/PB/2/11/87

Abolition of the Slave Trade and Slavery

The campaign for the abolition of the slave trade in the late eighteenth and early nineteenth centuries made use of petitions to Parliament on a scale not seen before. The petition from the inhabitants of Manchester in 1806, which had been encouraged by abolitionist Thomas Clarkson as a response to the petition against the Foreign Slave Trade Abolition Bill, was presented to the House of Lords on 14 May 1806, one day after a petition from the town's manufacturers and merchants. The Bill prevented the importation of slaves by British traders into territories belonging to foreign powers and was passed on 23 May. The petition is made up of nine sheets of parchment which have been stitched together and contains more than 2,000 names. In total the petition is over five metres long and the names include those of some women.

After the success of the 1806 Bill the stage was set for the full abolition of the British trade. The Prime Minister, Lord Grenville, introduced the Slave Trade Abolition Bill in the House of Lords on 2 January 1807 when it received a first reading. After consideration by the Lords the Bill arrived in the House of Commons on 10 February. William Wilberforce, after 18 years of promoting abolition, received a standing ovation during the key debate on 23 February. The debate lasted ten hours and the vote did not take place until four in the morning of the following day, when the House voted in favour of the Bill by 283 votes to 16 – a victory far in excess of expectations. The remaining stages took a further month to complete, and the Bill received Royal Assent on 25 March 1807.

Although the British ended their slave trade in 1807 slavery itself continued in the British colonies until full emancipation was achieved in 1833. The Bill to effect this received Royal Assent on 28 August 1833. The Act made provision for the payment of £20,000,000 in compensation to plantation owners but did not grant immediate freedom to the enslaved, establishing instead a system of apprenticeships.

85 Petition from the inhabitants of Manchester in support of the Foreign Slave Trade Abolition Bill, 14 May 1806
Parliamentary Archives, HL/PO/JO/10/8/106

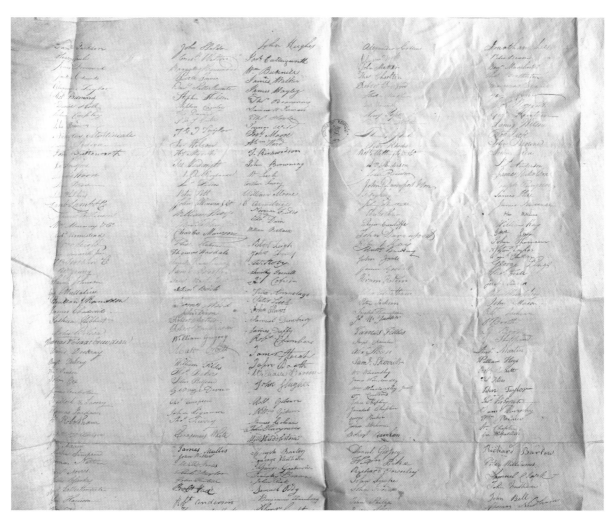

86 *An Act for the Abolition of the Slave Trade*, 47 George III session 1, c. 36, 1807
Parliamentary Archives, HL/PO/PU/1/1807/47G3s1n60

87 *An Act for the Abolition of Slavery throughout the British Colonies, for promoting the Industry of the manumitted Slaves, and for compensating the Persons hitherto entitled to the Services of such Slaves*, 3&4 William IV, c. 73, 1833
Parliamentary Archives, HL/PO/PU/1/1833/3&4W4n223

Assassination

The only assassination of a British Prime Minister took place on 11 May 1812 when Spencer Perceval was shot dead in the House of Commons Lobby. The perpetrator, John Bellingham, was a disgruntled and mentally unstable merchant who had been arrested for debt while on a business trip in Archangel and had spent five years in various rat-infested prisons in Russia, unable to obtain the help of the British Consul. On his release and return to England he had failed to get compensation from the Government or have the matter brought before Parliament. On the afternoon of 11 May 1812 his frustration boiled over and he waited at the entrance to the House of Commons Chamber with a pistol hidden in a secret pocket inside his greatcoat. Spencer Perceval died almost immediately from a fatal chest wound. Bellingham was tried three days later and went to the gallows on 18 May, still feeling fully justified in his actions to obtain redress for his grievances. These hastily scribbled notes contain the announcement to the House of Lords by the Lord Chancellor, hours after the shooting, who requested *That an humble address be presented to express to his Royal Highness the Prince Regent the Horror which this House feels at the atrociousness of the fact of the assassination of the Right Honourable Spencer Perceval within the walls of Parliament and humbly to entreat the HRH to direct all proper measures to be taken without delay for bringing the offender to Justice*.

88 Notes on the assassination of Spencer
Perceval, 11 May 1812
Parliamentary Archives, HL/PO/JO/10/8/276A

The Last Coronation Feast

The coronation of George IV on 19 July 1821 saw the King's return to public favour following the disastrous embarrassment of his attempt to remove the title of his wife, Queen Caroline, the previous year. The lavish celebrations cost Parliament some £243,000. Having fended off an attempt by the Queen to break into the Abbey during the ceremony, the King then attended what was to become the last-ever coronation feast in Westminster Hall. The Hall had been cleared of its temporary structures and two tiers of galleries were constructed which held thousands of invited guests, with illumination provided by chandeliers. At the north end, a thirty-foot triumphal Gothick arch had been constructed by the Office of Works, through which the King's Champion rode (on a circus horse used to crowds), to throw down the gauntlet in a final enactment of the medieval feasting ceremony for a new monarch. Officiating at the feast was the herald and antiquary Sir George Nayler. His magnificent colour plate book, *The History of the Coronation of George IV*, was illustrated by F P Stephanoff and others and published posthumously.

89 Ticket for the
Coronation Banquet in
Westminster Hall, 1821
Parliamentary Archives,
LGC/5/2/135

90 The King's champion
during the first course,
*History of the Coronation of
George IV* by G. Nayler, 1839
Parliamentary Archives,
LGC/8/1/11

The Longest Act

The longest Act held by the Parliamentary Archives is an Act passed in 1821 which appointed commissioners to collect the Land Tax. It is made up of 757 membranes and is estimated to be 348 metres long unrolled.

First introduced in 1693, the Land Tax was the first, and for many years the only, form of direct taxation to be levied on a regular basis in Great Britain. Essentially a tax on real estate and property, its collection was supervised by commissioners appointed by Acts of Parliament. During the eighteenth century the numbers of commissioners increased dramatically. The 1821 Act contains the names of approximately 65,000 commissioners which was the largest number ever appointed. It is possible that this was partly on account of a desire by the Treasury to maximise revenue at a time when the collection of the Land Tax was coming under scrutiny.

The Land Tax was finally abolished in 1963.

91 *An Act for appointing Commissioners for carrying into Execution an Act of this
Session of Parliament, for granting to His Majesty a Duty on Pensions and Offices
in England; and an Act, made in the Thirty eighth Year of His late Majesty, for
granting an Aid to His Majesty by a Land Tax to be raised in Great Britain,
for the Service of the Year One thousand seven hundred and ninety eight,*
1 & 2 George IV, c. 123, 1821
Parliamentary Archives, HL/PO/PU/1/1821/1&2G4n248

The Right to Vote

The passing of the Great Reform Act in 1832 was a mixture of political circumstance and popular pressure. The pro-reform Whig Lord Grey became Prime Minister in 1830 and agitation from extra-parliamentary radicals finally convinced a sceptical King and hostile Tory peers that reform was necessary. The effect of this Act was to enable the middle classes of the big industrial towns to share in political power. A uniform borough franchise was created, allowing adult males occupying property worth at least £10 a year to vote. In the counties the franchise was broadened to include the more substantial tenant farmers, small landowners and shopkeepers. Fifty-six towns with less than 2,000 inhabitants ('rotten boroughs') lost separate representation and 31 further towns were reduced to one MP. Sixty-seven new constituencies were created.

From the late 1830s to the 1850s the Chartist movement demanded further reform. In 1867 the Second Reform Act gave the vote to working class men for the first time, enfranchising all male householders in boroughs who paid rent of £10 a year or more and doubling the electorate from one million to two million. The Third Reform Act of 1884 extended the vote to householders in the counties, establishing a uniform adult male franchise throughout the country. In 1872 another significant reform took place with the Secret Ballot Act, which required that parliamentary elections be held by secret ballot, reducing the opportunity for elections to be influenced by bribery or intimidation.

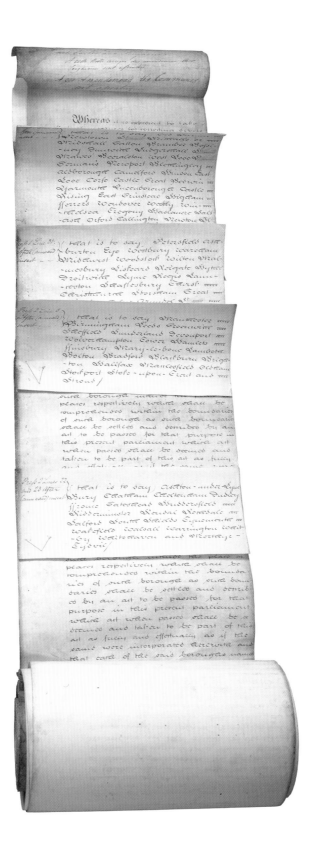

92 *An Act to amend the Representation of the People in England and Wales (the Great Reform Act),* 2&3 William IV, c. 45, 1832
Parliamentary Archives, HL/PO/PU/1/1832/2&3W4n147

93 *An Act further to amend the Laws relating to the Representation of the People in England and Wales* (the Second Reform Act), 30 & 31 Victoria I, c. 102, 1867
Parliamentary Archives, HL/PO/PU/1/1867/30&31V1n309

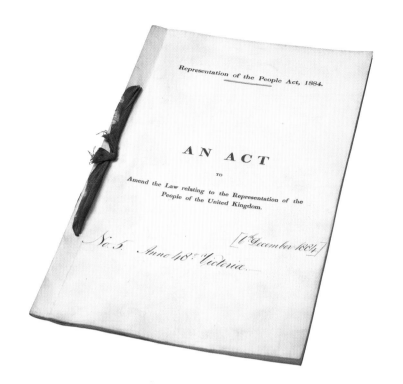

94 *An Act to amend the Law relating to the Representation of the People of the United Kingdom* (the Third Reform Act), 48 & 49 Victoria I, c. 3, 1884
Parliamentary Archives, HL/PO/PU/1/1884/48&49V1n5

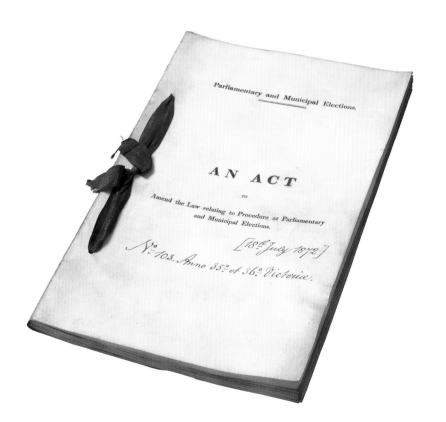

95 *An Act to amend the Law relating to Procedure at Parliamentary and Municipal Elections* (the Secret Ballot Act), 35 & 36 Victoria I, c. 33, 1872
Parliamentary Archives, HL/PO/PU/1/1872/35&36V1n103

The Great Fire of Westminster

At 6.30am on 16 October 1834, workmen began burning two cart loads of tally sticks in the central heating stoves under the House of Lords Chamber. Tally sticks were a form of receipt for government income used from the twelfth century to 1826, created by the Exchequer which was situated within the old Palace of Westminster. The furnaces were overstoked, causing a fire in the flues, and twelve hours later the two ancient Houses of Parliament were engulfed by a catastrophic blaze. Although Westminster Hall was saved, the core of the medieval Palace was a burnt-out shell by the following morning. All of the records of the House of Commons were destroyed except for 231 manuscript Journals and a few other survivals. These included an engrossed Commons' bill on hop duty (stored in error with the Lords' archives which remained unaffected by the fire) and two wage books from the Serjeant at Arms Office, licked by the flames – one has scorched pages and the other blistered covers. Eyewitness accounts abounded. One of the most compelling comes from Frances Rickman, daughter of John Rickman (Clerk Assistant in the Commons), who lived in the family home within the Palace, to the north-east of Westminster Hall. Writing to her absent sister about the disaster at 3.30am, her letter conjures up both the terror and amazement of that night and includes a sketch of the House of Commons in flames. A later letter enclosed a plan of the old Palace showing the extent of the destruction.

96 Tally sticks, *c.*1293–1294
Parliamentary Archives,
HL/PO/RO/1/195/4-6

97 Engrossed Commons'
bill to provide for more
convenient payment of the
excise duty on hops,
July 1828
Parliamentary Archives,
HL/PO/JO/10/8/783B

98 Scorched book of
receipts and payments
from the Serjeant at
Arms Office, 1813–1834
Parliamentary Archives,
HC/SA/SJ/9/55

99 Letter from Frances
Rickman to her sister Anne,
17 October 1834
Parliamentary Archives, RIC/1

Palace Yard
½ past 3 o'c A.M.

Thank God my dearest Anne after near eight hours dread-
ful doubt we seem all safe, tho' I am still partly lighted
by the still blazing House of Commons! — I fear you will
hear of the awful fire before this reaches you & have
been much alarmed for us; indeed. as you will imagine
it has been the most awful thing it is possible to con-
ceive. I will give you as collected an acc.t as I can for my
legs ache and I c.d not sleep so I may as well write. after
dinner at ½ past six this Eveng Papa & Mama taking a nap. in
came Ellis — "think Miss there's a small fire broke out at the
Ho. Lords." I said come to the leads with me to see it. & there
even then a volume of flame was blowing towards the Wilder.
Papa at first thought it w.d be got under but soon it fearfully
grew & we had little doubt the Hall would catch. the Ho. Lords
we c.d not see, but soon heard that it & Mr. Leys & the Library were
destroyed. then the flames burst from Ho. Commn: windows
& sooner than I c.d believe. the interior of that was destroyd—
now see my view. the West window in bow room my prospect:
front state rooms of   Speakers remain
entire; (outwardly) reld   flame   smoke. rises from
the quadrangle &   the open. Ho. Com: arches
(curvd like fountains   Abbey) are filled with an
orange light nearly the whole of S. End of Speakers is
destroyed—poor Papa will grieve for the Library. Mr. May

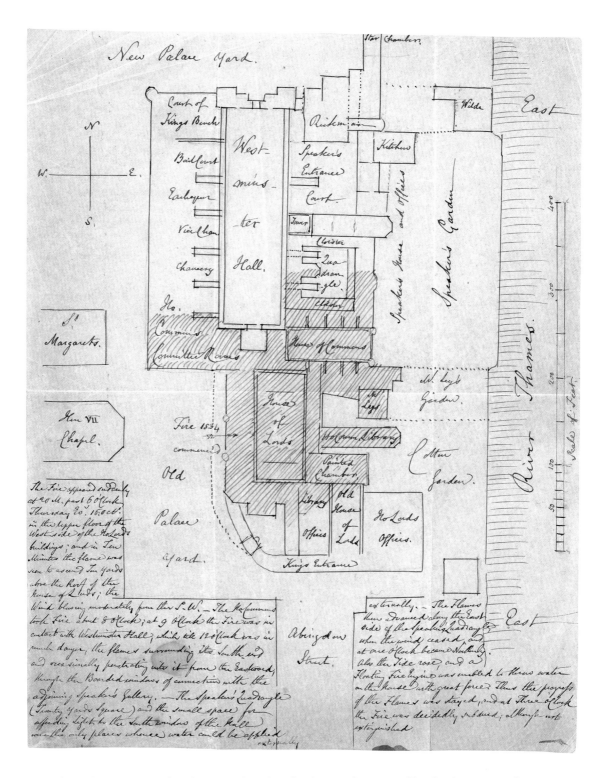

100 Plan of the Houses of Parliament showing the destruction caused by the fire, 20 October 1834
Parliamentary Archives, RIC/3

The New Palace of Westminster

Following a national competition to design a new Palace of Westminster after the 1834 fire, the Government awarded the contract to the architect Charles Barry. He enlisted the services of A W N Pugin as his designer. Together they created one of the most familiar and iconic buildings in the world and defined the archetypal style of the Victorian period: neo-gothic. This selection of items illustrates the mind-boggling detail of their joint creation.

The Edinburgh stained glass firm of Ballantine & Allan submitted designs in 1844 for a series of twelve windows (later reworked by Pugin), each portraying a period in British history. Shown here is the window for Edward I (1272–1307) to Edward III (1327–1377), including both those kings and their queens, but also with the unmistakeable figure of the poet Chaucer in the bottom right light. The ceremonial silver trowel was used by a relation of the builder to lay the first stone of the Clock Tower ('Big Ben') on 28 September 1845. From the opposite end of the Palace comes a section through the archway of the Sovereign's Entrance under the 'Royal Tower' – later renamed the Victoria Tower. Octavius Moulton-Barratt (brother of Elizabeth Barratt-Browning) was a junior draftsman in Charles Barry's office. His 'Gothic' portfolio of 1847 included many direct copies of original drawings by Pugin for ceiling coves in the Robing Room of the House of Lords, tile designs and more stained glass.

The Palace of Westminster was designated a World Heritage Site in 1987.

WINDOW Nº 5.

101 Stained glass designs
by Ballantine & Allan
of Edinburgh, 1844
Parliamentary Archives, BAD/5

102 Ceremonial silver
trowel, 1845
Parliamentary Archives,
OOW/50

103 Section through the
Sovereign's Entrance under
the Victoria Tower, *c.*1842
Parliamentary Archives, BAR/8

104 Copies by Octavius
Moulton-Barratt of designs
for the interior of the
Houses of Parliament,
after Pugin, 1847
Parliamentary Archives,
MOU/box5/238

Canada

The British North America Act of 1867, also known by Canadians as the Constitution Act, established Canada as a self-governing federation of four provinces: Nova Scotia, New Brunswick, Ontario and Quebec. Although each province retained its own separate local parliament under a lieutenant-governor, a parliament comprising a representative assembly and a nominated senate was created and met in Ottawa. The Act was designed to improve the ability of Canada to resist any possible aggression from the United States of America.

105 *An Act for the Union of Canada, Nova Scotia, and New Brunswick, and the Government thereof; and for Purposes connected therewith,*
30 & 31 Victoria I, c. 3, 1867
Parliamentary Archives, HL/PO/PU/1/1867/30&31V1n5

Women and Parliament

The Great Reform Act 1832 had enfranchised some men but explicitly denied the vote to women for the first time. The first petition from a woman asking for the vote was presented to the House of Commons in 1832 and from the 1860s a number of groups of women, known as suffragists, campaigned for the vote by the use of petitions. They were supported by some prominent male Members of Parliament including John Stuart Mill. In 1898 a national organisation was formed, the National Union of Women's Suffrage Societies, led by Millicent Garrett Fawcett. The petition from the Mistresses of Dulwich High School, which was presented during the passage of the Third Reform Act in 1884, is an excellent example of peaceful lobbying by professional women who paid taxes and therefore sought representation.

Although women did not obtain the vote during the nineteenth century, they did succeed in making other important legislative changes, to the divorce and matrimonial laws, for example, and to the law governing married women's property. Previously, everything a woman owned passed to her husband on her marriage. In 1870 the Married Women's Property Act enabled women to keep their own earnings and to inherit property and money; it is pictured here with subsequent Acts on the same subject.

106 *An Act to amend the Law relating to the Property of Married Women*, 33 & 34 Victoria I, c. 93, 1870
Parliamentary Archives, HL/PO/PU/1/1870/33&34V1n227

To the Right Honourable, the Lords Spiritual and Temporal of Great Britain and Ireland in Parliament assembled.

The humble Petition of the undersigned the Head Mistress & Assistant Mistresses of the Dulwich High School.

Sheweth

That a measure is now before Parliament for extending the Franchise to all men householders in the United Kingdom.

That by this Bill two millions of the least educated section of the Community will be added to the electorate, while educated and intelligent women, who are heads of households, are excluded from the operation of the Bill, although they contribute equally with men to the taxation of the Country.

That among the persons so excluded are women landowners, who form one seventh of the land-proprietors of the country; women of means and position living on their own property, schoolmistresses and other Teachers, women farmers, merchants manufacturers and shopkeepers, besides large numbers of self supporting women engaged in other occupations. They believe that the claim of these householders for admission within the pale of the Constitution is as reasonable as that of the County Householders, and that they would be at least equal in general and political intelligence to the great body of agricultural and other labourers who are to be enfranchised by the Government Bill.

That the injustice of excluding women householders from representation would be greatly intensified by the operation of the new service franchise, under which the servants of a Lady, living in houses for which she paid rent and taxes, would have the vote in right of the occupation of those houses while she herself though the head of the household would have no vote.

Wherefore your Petitioners humbly pray that in any measure which may be submitted to your Right Honourable House, for amending the Law relating to the Representation of the People, your Lordships will make such provision as shall seem expedient for the exercise of the Franchise by duly qualified women.

And your Petitioners will ever pray &c.

Mary Alys	High School for Girls, Dulwich		
L. T. Spencer	High School for Girls West Dulwich	Margaret Morison	High School for Girls W. Dulwich
Clara Arnold	High School for Girls W. Dulwich	Grace Bushnell	High School for Girls, W. Dulwich
Helen Amoro	High School for Girls W. Dulwich	Louise Brassine	High School for Girls W. Dulwich
Dora Knight	High School for Girls	Catherine A. Good	High School for Girls
Mary E. Swindells	High School for Girls	Mary A. Burrell	High School for Girls
Lenore Eversfield	High School for Girls	William Lynn	High School for Girls
Ida B. Hurrell	High School for Girls	Humphrey Stark M.B. Dun.	High School for Girls
Emily Collyns	High School for Girls		
Maud M. Escott	High School for Girls		
Anna Barth	High School for Girls		
Sarah Lukes	High School for Girls		
Gertrude Smith	High School for Girls		
Ida Salvage	High School for Girls		
Bertha J. Taylor	High School for Girls		
Alice Russell	High School for Girls		

107 Petition for votes for women from the Mistresses of Dulwich High School, 3 November 1884
Parliamentary Archives, HL/PO/6/11A

Whereas the women of the Nation have made clear t[...] their desire to possess the Parliamentary Vo[...]

[Wh]**ereas** working women, and women in the home, are [...] of the Vote since legislation is inte[r]fering m[...]

[...] the

[...]**EN'S FREEDOM** [...]

calls upon the Government to remove the sex [...] women of their just right of voting in the [...]

DEMAND [...]

the immedia**te** extension of the Franchise [...] it is, or may be enjoyed by men.

The Nation can never be free until the law [...]

VOTES FOR W[...]

THE DEMAND IS JUST.   THE REF[...]

DELAY IS UNWISE AND UNJU[...]

Therefore in the Name of Liberty and Humanity [...] claims the Vote

THIS SESS[...]

W. CONQUEST & Co., PRINTERS, TOTTENHAM.

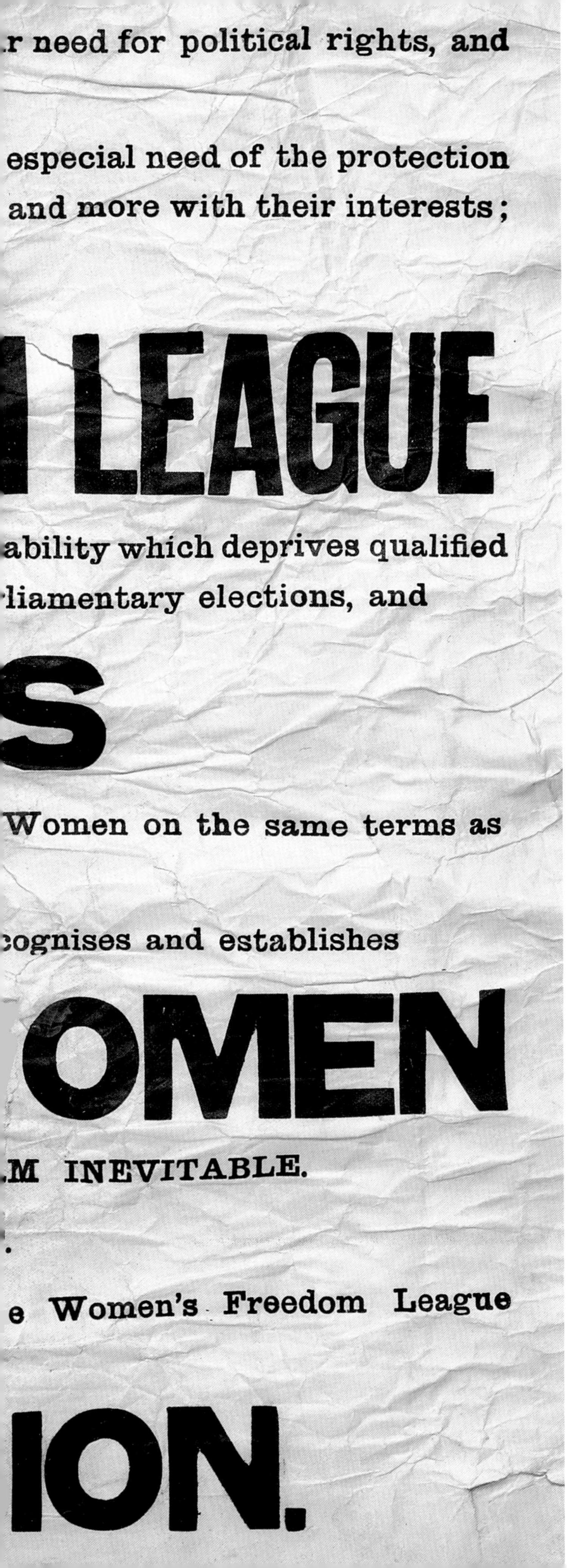

r need for political rights, **and**

especial need of the protection
and more with their interests;

LEAGUE

ability which deprives qualified
liamentary elections, and

S

Women on the same terms as

ognises and establishes

OMEN

M INEVITABLE.

.

e Women's Freedom League

ION.

The 20th Century

Parliament and Empire

During the nineteenth century Parliament passed legislation to provide for the government of the colonies in Australia. In the 1890s these colonies agreed to become a federation, a model that had been established for Canada in 1867. On 9 July 1900 Parliament passed the Commonwealth of Australia Constitution Act, which provided for a federation of six states overseen by a governor-general as the representative of the Monarch. The federation came into being on 1 January 1901.

As well as providing for colonial self-government, Parliament attempted to clarify the legislative relationship between itself and the Dominions, as colonies such as Australia, Canada and New Zealand became known. In 1931, by the Statute of Westminster, the British Parliament conceded its remaining authority over the Dominions to their own governments. The Act initially applied to the six Dominions which existed in 1931: Canada, Newfoundland, New Zealand, Australia, South Africa and the Irish Free State. The Act also assisted in formalising the concept of the Commonwealth of Nations.

108 Commission for
Royal Assent to the
Commonwealth of Australia
Constitution Act,
9 July 1900
Parliamentary Archives,
HL/PO/JO/10/3/295/10

109 *An Act to constitute the*
Commonwealth of Australia,
63 & 64 Victoria I,
c. 12, 1900
Parliamentary Archives,
HL/PO/PU/1/1900/63&64V1n61

110 *Statute of Westminster,*
c. 4, 1931
Parliamentary Archives,
HL/PO/PU/1/1931/22&23G5c4

Visitors on the Terrace

Members of both Houses frequently welcome important delegations and VIPs to the Palace of Westminster. The fine photographic collections of the Parliamentary Archives testify to the enduring appeal of tea on the sunny Terrace overlooking the River Thames. The photographs taken by the MP Benjamin Stone offer a fascinating glimpse of the Palace and its visitors in the early 1900s and, in this selection, honoured guests from across the Empire cutting a dash on the occasion of Edward VII's coronation in 1902. Another rich source of photographs, this time from the mid-twentieth century, is the collection of Gerald Pudsey, a prolific Westminster photographer who snapped many star-struck MPs and Peers with their guests from film and stage. A particularly fascinating encounter took place in 1955 between Bessie Braddock, the formidable Labour MP for Liverpool Exchange, and the Hollywood legend Marlene Dietrich who was on a cabaret tour during the summer of that year.

111 Indian army officers on the Terrace, July 1902
Parliamentary Archives, HC/LB/1/111/20/10

112 Bessie Braddock MP and Marlene Dietrich on the Terrace, 13 July 1955
Parliamentary Archives, PUD/14/100

Women's Suffrage

By the early 1900s some women had become frustrated that years of peaceful campaigning by groups such as the National Union of Women's Suffrage Societies had not yet obtained them the vote. They formed new associations which used more forceful and direct methods, and such women became known as suffragettes. They included Emmeline Pankhurst and her daughters Christabel, Adela and Sylvia, whose Women's Social and Political Union took part in a number of violent campaigns such as the 'rush' on Parliament in June 1908. Other well-known suffragettes included Emily Wilding Davison, who hid inside Parliament in a broom cupboard on census night in 1911, and who later died under the King's horse at the Derby in 1913.

On 28 October 1908 two suffragettes from the Women's Freedom League, Helen Fox and Muriel Matters, unfurled a banner from the Ladies' Gallery in the House of Commons. These women chained themselves to the grille over the window of the Gallery and had to be cut from it in a committee room. Their protest was one of three simultaneous suffragette demonstrations in Parliament that day, including one by men, as described in the police report on the incidents.

113 Suffragette banner,
28 October 1908
Parliamentary Archives,
HC/SA/SJ/3/1

28th October 1908

I have to report for information of the Sergt at Arms that at 8.30 pm a Demonstration took place in the Ladies Gallery and St Stephens Hall also the Members Gallery simultaneously by members of the Womens Freedom League.

The following had been taken to the Ladies Gallery at about 5.30 pm by Mr Stephen Collins MP.
Miss Helen Fox ⎱ 1 Robert St
" Muriel Matters ⎰ Adelphi WC
Both chained themselves to the ironwork of the grill and were brought out with the ironwork and the locks were filed off in a Committee Room. The following were ejected from St Stephens Hall
Miss Henderson
" E. Bremner

Miss A. Neilans
" M. Sidley
" May Taplin
" Mary Mammng
" Irene Tillard.

All behaving in a disorderly manner by shouting votes for Women, they had entered by asking for a member and 5 of them were in 2 lots for Mr Stephen Collins & Mr O'Grady MP but their cards had not time to reach the members before they became disorderly. The following were ejected from the members Gallery
Thomas Bayard Simmonds
Victor Starr for being disorderly Simmonds entered with an order from Mr Clynes MP. he was well known to Police and two plain clothes men sat on either side of him and he was ejected at once, Starr entered with an order from Mr W Crooks MP.

All being ejected from the Building in accordance with the Sergts instructions. The following of them were charged with offences committed outside after they had been ejected from the House

Muriel Matters (the one chained in Gallery)
Margurite Henderson
Edith Bremner ⎱ all ejected
Alison Neilson ⎰ from St
Mary Manning ⎰ Stephens Hall

Ten others were charged with offences outside, but we have no knowledge of them being here

Scantlebury
Ch Draper
Erskine Insp

114 Police report on activities
at the House of Commons,
28 October 1908
Parliamentary Archives,
HC/SA/SJ/10/12

Universal Franchise

An Act to reform the electoral system was deemed necessary during the First World War as millions of returning soldiers were not entitled to the vote because of property and residential qualifications. The Representation of the People Act of 1918 widened suffrage by abolishing almost all property qualifications for men and enfranchising women over 30 who met minimum property qualifications. The Act also brought in the present system of holding general elections on one day and introduced an annual electoral register. These changes saw the size of the electorate triple from 7.7 million to 21.4 million. Women now accounted for about 43% of the electorate.

Women, however, were still not equal to men in terms of the franchise, as men could vote from the age of 21. The requirement to be 30 years old or more was to ensure that women did not form the majority of the electorate; if women had been enfranchised on the same terms as men, they would have been in the majority because of the loss of men in the war. Ten years later the Equal Franchise Act was passed *'for the purpose of providing that the parliamentary franchise shall be the same for men and women'*. It lowered the voting age for women to 21, giving the vote to five million women. Men and women now had the same qualifications based on residence, business premises, or being the spouse of a person with a business premises qualification.

115 *Representation of the People Act*, c. 64, 1918
Parliamentary Archives, HL/PO/PU/1/1918/7&8G5c64

Le Roy le veult.

CHAPTER 12.

An Act to assimilate the franchises for men and women in respect of parliamentary and local government elections; and for purposes consequential thereon. [2nd July 1928.]

A.D. 1928.
———

BE it enacted by the King's most Excellent Majesty, by and with the advice and consent of the Lords Spiritual and Temporal, and Commons, in this present Parliament assembled, and by the authority of the same, as follows :—

1. For the purpose of providing that the parliamentary franchise shall be the same for men and women, subsections (1) and (2) of section four of the Representation of the People Act, 1918 (in this Act referred to as " the principal Act ") shall be repealed and the following sections shall be substituted for sections one and two of that Act :—

Assimilation of parliamentary franchise of men and women. 7 & 8 Geo. 5. c. 64.

(Section to be substituted for the said section one.)

" .—(1) A person shall be entitled to be registered as a parliamentary elector for a constituency (other than a university constituency), if he or she is of full age and not subject to any legal incapacity; and

(*a*) has the requisite residence qualification; or

(*b*) has the requisite business premises qualification; or

A 2   1

116 *Representation of the People (Equal Franchise) Act*, c. 12, 1928
Parliamentary Archives, HL/PO/PU/1/1928/18&19G5c12

Women in Parliament

The first woman to be elected to Parliament was Constance Markiewicz in the General Election of 1918, the first election at which some women could vote. As a member of Sinn Fein, Markiewicz never took her seat. The first woman to take her seat in Parliament was Nancy Astor, Conservative MP for Plymouth Sutton 1919–1945. She was elected in a by-election, replacing her husband Waldorf Astor after his elevation to the peerage. Nancy Astor had never been involved in the suffrage campaign, but she worked unfailingly to promote women's causes in the House of Commons. She was soon joined by the first Liberal woman MP in 1921, Margaret Wintringham, and the first Labour women MPs, Susan Lawrence, Margaret Bondfield and Dorothy Jewson, who were all elected in 1923.

The number of women MPs increased very slowly but had reached 24 by the time Margaret 'Peggy' Herbison became Labour MP for North Lanarkshire in 1945. The items pictured here form a snapshot of her desk in the mid-1950s showing her diary, briefcase and coin purse. It is not known why they were abandoned in her desk, but they were found together with some of her papers when the desk was retrieved from storage in 2005.

117 Nancy Astor election
campaign leaflet, 1919
Parliamentary Archives, BRO/1

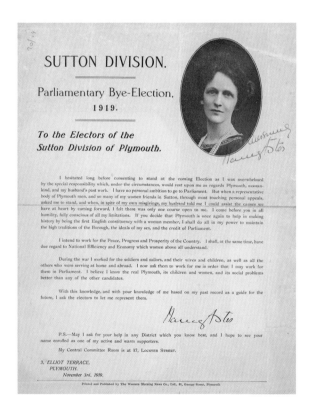

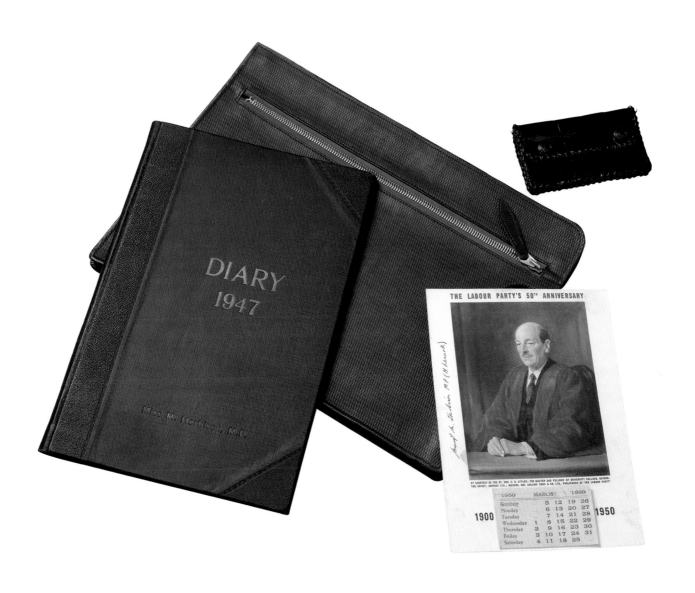

118 Personal items belonging to Margaret Herbison MP, 1950s
Parliamentary Archives, HER/11

Roof Restoration

Between 1913 and 1922 the incredible hammer-beam roof of Westminster Hall underwent a major restoration after its timbers had been found to be in a state of near collapse due to damage by death-watch beetle. The architect Sir Frank Baines drew up 38 technical 'schedules' illustrating the construction of the roof to aid his repairs. Accompanying them was a published report on the condition of the Hall's roof timbers. Lionel Earle, the Permanent Secretary to the Office of Works, commented on Baines' achievement: '*every word of the report and also the detail of the drawings show evidence of the stupendous care which has been taken in preparing it. I only hope that means will be found to allow both Houses of Parliament and the Treasury to see for themselves the care bestowed by Mr Baines and others on an important work of this kind*'. These magnificent drawings constitute a major source for one of the supreme masterpieces of medieval architecture, shedding light on the technological and artistic genius of Hugh Herland, the master carpenter who designed and built the roof for Richard II from 1394 to 1399.

119 Schedules to the report on the condition of the roof timbers of Westminster Hall by Sir Frank Baines, 1914
Parliamentary Archives, HC/LB/1/114/42

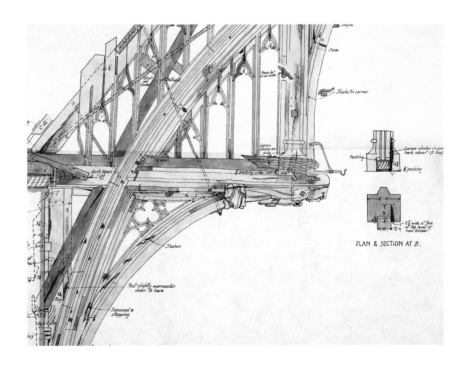

No 32

WESTMINSTER
HALL ROOF
PERSPECTIVE SHOWING
NEW STEELWORK

Ceremony and Uniform

Ceremony is an integral part of the work of Parliament and of the state functions that take place in connection with its activities. The office of Lord Great Chamberlain dates back to the eleventh century and, as the representative of the Crown's interest in the Royal Palace of Westminster, the postholder began to exercise influence over the running of the building and its affairs from at least the seventeenth century. These duties changed fundamentally when, in 1965, the Queen transferred to each House of Parliament that part of the Palace which it occupied, although the Lord Great Chamberlain retained custody of certain specific areas.

The records and objects to be found in the Lord Great Chamberlain's collection reflect these roles and responsibilities and their close relationship with those of Black Rod, who is Secretary to the Lord Great Chamberlain. They include a ceremonial sword and a hat worn by Redcoat.

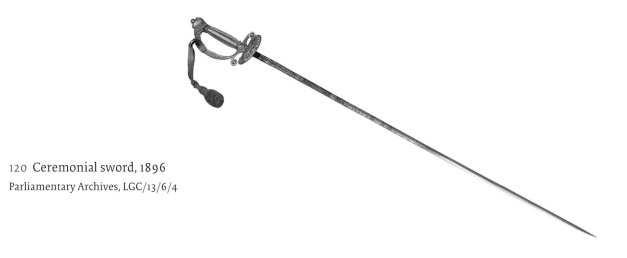

120 Ceremonial sword, 1896
Parliamentary Archives, LGC/13/6/4

121 Hat worn by Redcoat whilst
on duty at the Peers' Entrance at
the House of Lords, 20th cent.
Parliamentary Archives, LGC/13/6/2

The Highest Court

For centuries the House of Lords performed a judicial function as a court
of appeal and as such was the highest court in the land. The Appellate
Jurisdiction Act of 1876 established salaried Lords of Appeal in Ordinary
(Law Lords), who were life peers holding Letters Patent from the Crown.
The cases heard by the House of Lords ranged over many issues and
included the famous Donoghue v Stevenson case of 1932. This concerned
a snail found in a bottle of ginger beer, and the resulting judgment
established the principle of a duty of care. Another case focused on the
infringement of vacuum cleaner patents in 1912, the papers for which are
a novel source for the history of domestic appliances.

The judicial function of the House of Lords ended in 2009 when it was
transferred to the new Supreme Court.

122 Appeal Case papers,
London and South Western
Railway v British
Vacuum Cleaner
Company Limited, 1912
Parliamentary Archives,
HL/PO/JU/4/3/606

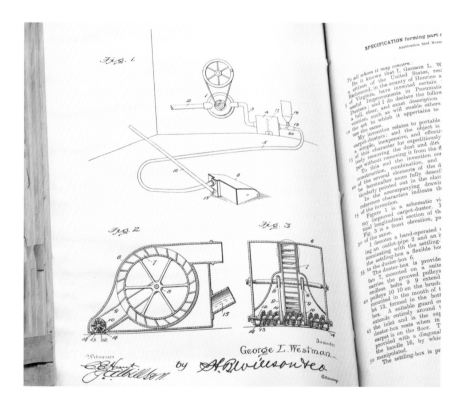

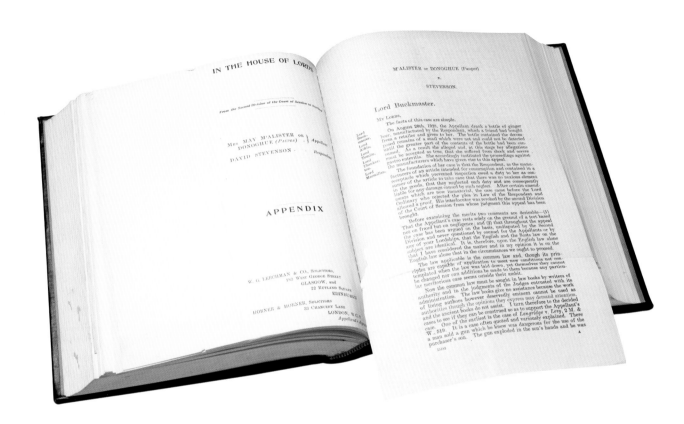

123 Appeal Case papers, McAlister (Donoghue), May v Stevenson, David, 1932
Parliamentary Archives, HL/PO/JU/4/3/873

The Abdication Crisis

On the death of King George V in 1936 his eldest son succeeded as King Edward VIII. He came to the throne on 20 January 1936, and signed the accession declaration. Edward's proposal to marry the twice-divorced American Wallis Simpson, however, provoked widespread opposition in the Government and across the Commonwealth. After much consideration, Prime Minister Stanley Baldwin advised the King that the Government would not support his marriage.

Rather than give Wallis Simpson up, Edward chose to abdicate. His message to the House of Lords in November 1936 said: *'I will not enter now into my private feelings, but I would beg that it should be remembered that the burden which constantly rests on the shoulders of a Sovereign is so heavy that it can only be borne in circumstances different from those in which I find myself'*. He formally ceased to be King on 11 December 1936. His brother, who succeeded him as King George VI, conferred the Dukedom of Windsor on him and he married Mrs Simpson in 1937.

124 Accession declaration of King Edward VIII, 20 January 1936
Parliamentary Archives, HL/PO/JO/10/10/1144A

I, EDWARD THE EIGHTH do solemnly and sincerely in the presence of God profess, testify, and declare that I am a faithful Protestant, and that I will, according to the true intent of the enactments which secure the Protestant succession to the Throne of my Realm, uphold and maintain the said enactments to the best of my powers according to law.

Edward RI

125 Message of abdication of King Edward VIII, 3 November 1936
Parliamentary Archives, HL/PO/JO/10/10/1146A

The Second World War

After the outbreak of the Second World War in 1939, a force of over 100 volunteers was quickly recruited to the Parliamentary detachment of the Local Defence Volunteers (the 'Home Guard'). Individuals who volunteered to join the Palace of Westminster Company were mostly men with previous war experience. By March 1943 more than 400 people were employed in the civil defence of the Palace under the supervision of the Air Raid Precautions Committee. The metal protective helmet pictured was one of the items of kit issued as part of these preparations, whilst the small black lamp belonged to the House of Commons Librarian, Strathearn Gordon. It is hooded to deflect light downwards during blackouts.

The LDV took part in Palace fire-watching and sentry duties in addition to manning a gun at the exit to Westminster underground station and taking responsibility for anti-tank measures on Westminster Bridge. Despite their best efforts to protect the building, the Palace was bombed a number of times during the war, most notably in May 1941 when the House of Commons Chamber was destroyed.

126 Protective helmet issued by Air Raid Precautions Committee, 1940s
Parliamentary Archives, HL/PO/3/18

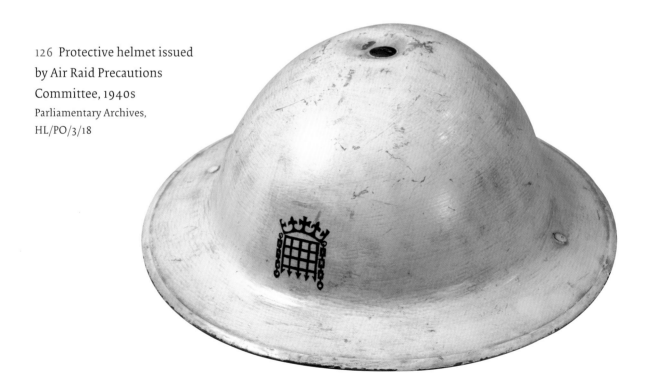

127 The House of Commons Librarian's
wartime bicycle lamp, 1940s
Parliamentary Archives,
HL/PO/3/17

128 Photographs of the bombed House of Commons Chamber, 1941
Parliamentary Archives, ARC/VAR/12

House of Lords Reform

Nineteenth-century parliamentary reform had affected the House of Commons but left the House of Lords untouched. The twentieth century, however, saw considerable changes to the powers and composition of the second chamber. The first significant change was triggered by the Lords' rejection of Lloyd George's 'People's Budget' in 1909 and the subsequent agreement of George V to create, if necessary, hundreds of new Liberal peers to neutralise the Conservative majority in the Upper House. In the event it was not necessary and the Lords passed, by a narrow 131–114 vote, the Parliament Act of 1911 which asserted the supremacy of the House of Commons by limiting the powers of the House of Lords to block legislation. Additionally, the maximum permitted time between general elections was reduced from seven to five years. In 1949 another Parliament Act reduced the delaying power of the Lords to one year.

In 1958 the composition of the House of Lords was changed by the Life Peerages Act. This enabled the creation of life peers other than Law Lords and allowed women to sit in the House for the first time. By virtue of the Act, four women took their seats in the House of Lords as life peers that year: Baroness Swanborough, Baroness Wootton of Abinger, Baroness Elliot of Harwood and Baroness Ravensdale of Kedleston. Further reforms followed in 1963 but the hereditary element in the Lords remained until all but 92 of their number were removed by the House of Lords Act of 1999.

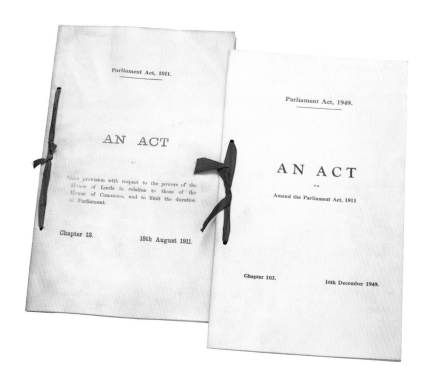

129 *Parliament Act,*
c. 13, 1911
Parliamentary Archives,
HL/PO/PU/1/1911/1&2G5c13

130 *Parliament Act,*
c. 103, 1949
Parliamentary Archives,
HL/PO/PU/1/1949/12,13&14G6c103

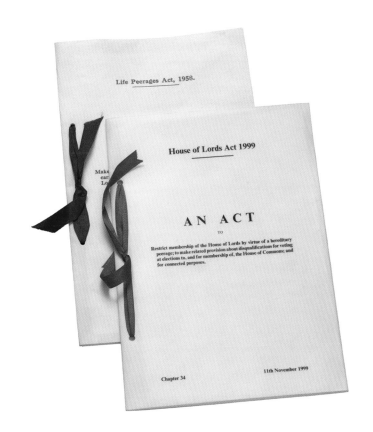

131 *Life Peerages Act,*
c. 21, 1958
Parliamentary Archives,
HL/PO/PU/1/1958/6&7Eliz2c21

132 *House of Lords Act,*
c. 34, 1999
Parliamentary Archives,
HL/PO/PU/1/1999/c34

HM Queen Elizabeth II

Queen Elizabeth II came to the throne in 1952, succeeding her father King George VI, and made the following declaration required by the Sovereign on accession: '*I, Elizabeth do solemnly and sincerely in the presence of God profess, testify, and declare that I am a faithful Protestant, and that I will, according to the true intent of the enactments which secure the Protestant succession to the Throne, uphold and maintain the said enactments to the best of my powers according to law*'. This text had been set out by the Accession Declaration Act of 1910, replacing the oath which was previously required under the Bill of Rights and the Act of Settlement.

Since 1952 the Queen has celebrated her Silver and Golden Jubilees and addressed Members of the House of Lords and House of Commons on both occasions.

133 Accession declaration of Queen Elizabeth II, 4 November 1952
Parliamentary Archives, HL/PO/JO/10/11/247A

I, ELIZABETH do solemnly and sincerely in the presence of God profess, testify, and declare that I am a faithful Protestant, and that I will, according to the true intent of the enactments which secure the Protestant succession to the Throne, uphold and maintain the said enactments to the best of my powers according to law.

Elizabeth R

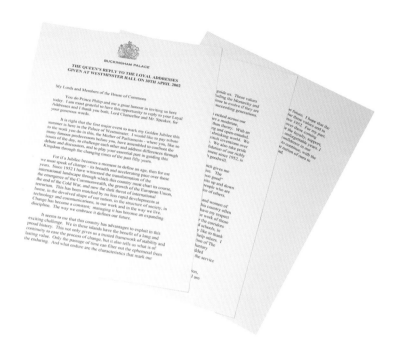

Left:

134 The Queen's address to Members of the House of Lords and House of Commons on the occasion of her Silver Jubilee, 4 May 1977

Parliamentary Archives, HL/PO/JO/10/11/1912/1116

Right:

135 The Queen's address to Members of the House of Lords and House of Commons on the occasion of her Golden Jubilee, 30 April 2002

Parliamentary Archives, HL/PO/JO/10/15/52/2266A

Unusual Evidence

In 1978 the House of Commons Select Committee on Science and
Technology undertook an inquiry into contingency arrangements for
dealing with oil pollution, following the wrecking of the oil tanker Eleni V.
The Eleni V was damaged in a collision in thick fog in the North Sea in May
1978 and up to 5,000 tonnes of heavy fuel oil were spilled. Some oil reached
the shoreline near Great Yarmouth in Norfolk. The Committee took written
evidence and examined witnesses from the Government and from local
councils. Amongst the evidence they collected was a specimen taken from
the oil slick, one of the more unusual items in the Parliamentary Archives.

136 Specimen of oil slick
from the Eleni V, 1978
Parliamentary Archives,
HC/CP/4417

Equality and Diversity

Sir Mancherjee Merwanjee Bhownaggree was Conservative MP for Bethnal Green between 1895 and 1906. Bhownaggree was born in Bombay, India, where he lived until he came to England in 1882 to study law. Knighted in 1892, he was one of the earliest Members of Parliament to come from an minority ethnic background (following Dadabhai Naoroji, Liberal MP for Finsbury Central 1892–1895).

David Thomas Pitt was created a life peer as Baron Pitt of Hampstead in 1975, only the second black Member of the House of Lords (the first being Learie Constantine, created Baron Constantine of Maraval and Nelson in 1969). Pitt was born in Grenada, studied medicine in Edinburgh, and lived and worked in Trinidad and the Caribbean before coming to London in 1947 where he established himself as an esteemed general practitioner, a champion of migrant communities and a campaigner against race discrimination. He stood for election to the House of Commons several times but was unsuccessful.

During the last quarter of the twentieth century, various landmark Acts of Parliament were passed to combat discrimination on grounds of race, sex or disability. The Human Rights Act of 1998 came into force in 2000, aiming to give effect to the European Convention on Human Rights.

137 Sir Mancherjee Merwanjee Bhownaggree MP, 1895
Parliamentary Archives, PHO/5/1/9

138 Baron Pitt of Hampstead, *c.*1976
Parliamentary Archives, HL/PO/1/595/12

139 *Sex Discrimination Act*, c. 65, 1975
Parliamentary Archives, HL/PO/PU/1/1975/c65

140 *Race Relations Act*, c. 74, 1976
Parliamentary Archives, HL/PO/PU/1/1976/c74

141 *Disability Discrimination Act*, c. 50, 1995
Parliamentary Archives, HL/PO/PU/1/1995/c50

142 *Human Rights Act*, c. 42, 1998
Parliamentary Archives, HL/PO/PU/1/1998/c42

Ireland, Scotland and Wales

The Government of Ireland Act of 1920 partitioned Ireland in two. 'Southern Ireland' was to have a devolved parliament in Dublin and 'Northern Ireland', a devolved parliament in Belfast. Both parts of Ireland were to continue sending representatives to the Westminster Parliament. Under the Anglo-Irish Treaty of December 1921, however, 'Southern Ireland' gained dominion status as the Irish Free State, whilst the six counties in Ulster remained part of the United Kingdom. In 1949 Acts passed by the British and Irish Parliaments recognised the Irish Free State as a republic.

The Parliament of Northern Ireland was abolished in 1973. There were subsequent assemblies in Northern Ireland for short periods of time and the current Northern Ireland Assembly was set up by Act of Parliament in 1998. After referenda were held, Acts also established a devolved Scottish Parliament and a National Assembly for Wales.

143 *Government of Ireland Act,* c. 67, 1920
Parliamentary Archives, HL/PO/PU/1/1920/10&11G5c67

Above left:

144 *Government of Wales Act,*
c. 38, 1998
Parliamentary Archives,
HL/PO/PU/1/1998/c38

Above right:

145 *Scotland Act,* c. 46, 1998
Parliamentary Archives,
HL/PO/PU/1/1998/c46

Left:

146 *Northern Ireland Act,*
c. 47, 1998
Parliamentary Archives,
HL/PO/PU/1/1998/c47

The Archives

The House of Lords began using the Victoria Tower as a record repository
from 1864, while the Commons' records gradually trickled in after 1927.
At the outbreak of World War II, most of the records were evacuated first
to Elstree, then to Laverstoke House in Hampshire. During their time in
the damp conditions there, they were affected by a serious mould outbreak.
This provided the impetus for an idea which had first been mooted in 1937:
the creation of a dedicated office within Parliament to actively manage its
record holdings. In 1946 the House of Lords Record Office was established
to care for the records of Parliament and make them available to the public.
In 2006 the office – by now a shared service of both Houses of Parliament
and involved in modern records management as well as historic
curation – was renamed the Parliamentary Archives.

147 View of the Victoria
Tower from the south,
looking up Millbank before
house clearances, 1905
Parliamentary Archives, FAR/1

148 Flagmen on top of the Victoria Tower, 1905
Parliamentary Archives, FAR/1

149 Maurice Bond OBE (Clerk of the Records 1946–1981) at his desk in the House of Lords Record Office, 1954
Parliamentary Archives, PIC/P/224

The 21st
Century

An Act of the New Millennium

The Freedom of Information Act of 2000 was one of the first Acts of the new millennium. It gave members of the public the right to request any information, with a few exemptions, held by a wide range of UK public authorities. Unusually, it specifically included by name the administrations of the House of Commons and the House of Lords among the bodies subject to the Act. It came into force on 1 January 2005 and its application had far-reaching consequences for both Government and Parliament.

Freedom of Information Act
2000

AN ACT

TO

Make provision for the disclosure of information held by public authorities or by persons providing services for them and to amend the Data Protection Act 1998 and the Public Records Act 1958; and for connected purposes.

30th November 2000

Chapter 36

150 *Freedom of Information Act*, c. 36, 2000
Parliamentary Archives, HL/PO/PU/1/2000/c36

Acknowledgements

We would like to acknowledge the support and assistance of the following:
Lara Artemis, Renee Brownsey-Joyce, Steve Chamberlain, Caroline Chipperfield,
Chris Clarke, Mark Collingwood, Mark Collins, Alison Couch, Kate Emms,
Vasilis Gialias, Simon Gough, Tim Green, Frances Grey, Liz Hallam Smith,
Benet Hiscock, Kevan Holland, Lois Jolly, Ted Lloyd-Jukes, Antony Makinson,
Tom McCarthy, Michael Mitchell, Sheila Mitchell, Fred Pace, Liz Parratt,
Annie Pinder, Melanie Unwin, Isolde Victory, Susan Wightman, Chris Williams,
Owen Williams and everyone at the Parliamentary Archives.

Contacting the Parliamentary Archives

Information on our public services is available at: www.parliament.uk/archives

To make an appointment to consult records in our Search Room
or to make an enquiry contact us at:

Parliamentary Archives
Houses of Parliament
London SW1A 0PW
United Kingdom

Email: archives@parliament.uk

Tel: 020 7219 3074

We are open all year round, Monday to Friday.

Index

The treasures are referenced by their sequential number